The Lost Suitcase

Also by Nicholas Delbanco

The Lost Suitcase

REFLECTIONS ON THE LITERARY LIFE

Nicholas Delbanco

COLUMBIA UNIVERSITY PRESS   NEW YORK

COLUMBIA UNIVERSITY PRESS

Publishers Since 1893

New York   Chichester, West Sussex

Copyright © 2000 Nicholas Delbanco

Library of Congress Cataloging-in-Publication Data

Delbanco, Nicholas.

The lost suitcase : reflections on the literary life /
Nicholas Delbanco.

p. cm.

ISBN 0–231–11542–3 (cloth)

ISBN 0–231–11543–1 (paper)

I. Title.

PS3554.E442L67   2000

818.′5403—DC21   99–28798

Casebound editions of Columbia University Press books are
printed on permanent and durable acid-free paper.

Printed in the United States of America

c 10 9 8 7 6 5 4 3 2 1

p 10 9 8 7 6 5 4 3 2 1

For Jon Manchip White

Heureux qui, comme Ulysse,
a fait un beau voyage

Contents

Acknowledgments

These essays were first published, often in substantially different form, in the following: "Travel, Art, and Death" in *The Georgia Review*; "Judgment" in *Writers on Writing*, eds. R. Pack and J. Parini, University Press of New England; "Rumford: His Book" in *Michigan Quarterly Review*; "Telephone" in *Salmagundi*; "Letter to a Young Fiction Writer" as "Dear Franz K" in *Letters to a Fiction Writer*, ed. F. Busch, W. W. Norton & Co.; "A Prayer for the Daughters" in *Fathering Daughters*, eds. D. Henry & J. McPherson, Beacon Press; "Less and More" in *How We Want to Live*, eds. S. Shreve and P. Shreve, Beacon Press; "Scribble, Scribble, Scribble" in *Harper's Magazine*. Early versions of chapters I and IV of "The Lost Suitcase" appeared, respectively, in *The Southern California Anthology* and *The Seattle Review*.

Travel, Art, and Death

For the past several years I've kept a kind of notebook—what others might call a commonplace book, a compilation of jottings—in the drawer of my desk. These are the stories that never quite attain fictive fruition, the speeches that don't reach the podium or print, the by-blows and commentaries that keep writers working, when not at real work. They are what Virginia Woolf described as "little darlings," the fine phrases and false starts and tangents and scenes from the cutting-room floor.

A writer's finished product always resembles his or her own other productions more closely than those of anyone else; we leave our fingerprints on every page. By their commas ye shall know them, and by their usage of the semicolon and the subordinate clause. So these entries have clustered almost as if by molecular affinity into characteristic groupings. They address the three great topics: travel, art, and death. Of another three great topics, politics, food, and sex, I seem here to have little to say. Or—to take another triad—on the subjects of hunting, memory, and taxes, I remain more or less mum. These particular "commonplaces" or "night thoughts" (the French might more grandly call them *pensées*) have been shaped and rearranged only a little—not so much to render these informal entries coherent as to make them in some formal way cohere.

What follows is a set of notes on motion, immobility, and the articulate effort to mediate between them: *travel, death,* and *art.*

We have, I think, an increasingly complicated sense of what it takes to live the simple life. The famous meal in Omar Khayyám's poem consists of "a jug of wine, a loaf of bread, and thou beside me in the wilderness." That original feast also entailed, it appears, a leg of lamb—but the translator of *The Rubáiyát,* Edward FitzGerald, thought mutton insufficiently romantic for a lovers' picnic and, as a good Victorian, simply omitted the meat. But what about olives, a hard-boiled egg or two, some vegetable munchies, cold fried chicken, and the Bloody Mary requisite for a tailgate collocation? It's hard to know, I mean, when enough's enough.

My wife and I, last autumn, took a trip to Greece. We spent a vivid week in that region of the Peloponnesus known as the Deep Mani, the southernmost tip of the land mass below the Bay of Corinth. It's not far from the high ring of stones in the ancient town of Mikinis that once sheltered the doomed House of Atreus. Nearby lies that splendid theater Epidaurus, where the tragedies of Agamemnon and Oedipus and their troubled progeny are still, every summer, performed. Yet the Mani has no cultural locus as such, no famous site to which tourists flock, no grand hotels facing the Acropolis; it's an empty and, to a degree, forbidding place. The olive and the orange tree look less firmly rooted than the prickly pear.

There are Byzantine chapels and hillside shrines, but little to evoke "the glory that was Greece." The Museum of the Mani displays photographs, not statuary or pottery shards, and the statistics as to literacy, sobriety, life expectancy, and so forth are not good. The roads are steep and switchbacked; erosion and tree felling and centuries of goats have left the mountains barren, a mixture of red dirt and shale. The Maniots are famous for their quarrelsome independence; this region has never been conquered, and its characteristic structure—a stone tower, sometimes as high as five stories—appears to have been, for centuries, built for the sake of toppling. The local blood feuds are fierce. You knock down your neighbor's tower, and then he levels yours.

Elena and I stayed in the near-deserted village of Vathia, in one of those ruined towers. The site is breathtaking: high on a crag, with the Aegean in the middle distance and the *kakavouna*, or "evil mountains," behind. A high wind howled; at night it rained. This was late October, and the restaurant in Vathia had shut down for the season. In that settlement the one phone had failed to operate for weeks; electricity proved chancy and hot water rare. The young have fled to Athens, where there's nightlife and work. Those who stay behind are elderly, and the women all wear black. They keep some chickens and perhaps a goat for milk; the men drink coffee and ouzo and play cards and board games noisily in the café. They pass the time in a manner not wholly comprehensible to this hurried, harried Westerner; in turn, time has passed them by.

I don't mean to compose one of those platitudinous sermons on the virtues of the "simple life," because it's by no means clear to me that their life and lot are easy or—if given the option—that they would reject a trade. But what these folk expect seems far closer to what they get than is the case for most of us; the distance, as it were, between ambition and achievement looms less large. An old woman in the water, with her slippers on and skirt hiked up, was anchoring her evening meal—a fish in a string bag—with rocks. That way it would keep fresh, salt-laved till cooking

time; she would have, no doubt, a jug of wine, and there
would be bread.

The photographs of generations previous are almost always
unsmiling; when you're asked to hold a pose it's hard to hold
a grin. Daguerre and his disciples took some time to complete their images, but standard equipment nowadays offers
split-second exposures and instantaneous results. We've all
been told to "smile" or "say 'cheese,' " to flash our white
teeth at the camera's eye; it's only the professional beauty—
the actor, say, or model—who's allowed to look earnest and
tight-lipped on film. So a family album can tend to mislead,
as though life has always been a perpetual vacation with
everyone all the time happy and gathered—arms linked—in
convivial groups. Our recent visual history establishes a
record of posed protracted bliss.

This is of course not the case. Even the best-humored
and most fortunate among us spend less time smiling than
photos suggest, and the true family album should also
record pain and loss. Divorce grows as common as marriage,
but we fail to take pictures of that ceremony and its parti-
cipants after a session in court. Death is the inevitable consequence of birth, but how many "final" photographs adorn
the book that starts with a baby picture and announcement?
In every child's box of mementoes there's likely to be a
scrawled declaration of hatred for siblings or dinner or
school, a farewell note announcing, "I've just run away!"
But the photographs will be of birthday parties or Hal-
loween costumes or the little darling gussied up for the first
day of school or first dance. . . .

A friend of mine collects paintings and engravings that
feature, on a table or bookshelf, a skull; it seems a strange
sort of hobby to have, but as he accurately says, the grin-
ning skull, *memento mori*, has long been an emblem of
life. When Hamlet says, "Alas, poor Yorick," and converses
with that bit of unearthed bone, he's following hallowed
tradition.

Walk through any portrait gallery that features folk from the unrecent past and you'll receive that same grave glare, that sense of transience stayed. And the lips of the cleric or lady or king are sealed not merely—though no doubt in part—because their teeth were bad. As a character in *Troilus and Cressida* reminds us, "Time hath, my lord, a wallet at his back, wherein he puts alms for oblivion." Smile.

Recently two of my "masters" have died. I use the word with some particularity; they were my much-respected teachers, though I took no formal class from either and did not know them well. Nor, to my knowledge, were they particularly close colleagues; Wallace Stegner lived in California and Vermont, John Hersey in Martha's Vineyard and Key West. But they are neighbors now in what James Baldwin—another late lamented master—called "the royal fellowship of death."

Among that fellowship these two new arrivals will surely be made welcome and acknowledged. They were prolific novelists who each produced consequential journalism, short fiction, and memoirs. They wrote about Hiroshima and bluefishing and the vanishing Old West and principles of conservation and strategies of prose. They were "men of letters" in a fashion that seems these days more and more rare. The privacy-loving Hersey was reserved to the point of seeming-shyness; he had been born in China, and something of the Mandarin remained. Stegner too seemed ill at ease in coat and tie or at the podium, as if he'd rather be sitting a horse. Yet both commanded full attention when they spoke. They had long careers, both, and died in the fullness of time; Hersey was approaching eighty and Stegner was well past that age.

I don't propose to furnish here an obituary notice—this is not a day-after account of lives lost—nor will I list all their publications, much less describe what their legacy might mean. *The Big Rock Candy Mountain, The Spectator Bird, Hiroshima, The Algiers Motel Incident, Crossing to Safety,*

A Single Pebble, All the Little Live Things, Fling, A Bell for Adano—how could one hope to compass the various achievements of these two so-various writers? There have been memorial services and articles sufficient in any case. But these authors seemed to me while living to have a kind of indestructibility, and I want to honor their passing by reminding myself once more of what endures.

These thoughts have been occasioned by a funeral I did recently attend. My dead mother's elder brother died at eighty-six. He had been in failing and then failed health for years; his own "crossing to safety" was nearly imperceptible, and the funeral service was private and brief. I flew to New York City in order to pay, as they say, "my respects," and at the service found out much about the man I had either forgotten or never quite known. He once sang Cherubino, for instance, as a dandy in Berlin; he played the violin but gave it up when Hitler came to power and never touched the instrument again. When young and robust in the Second World War, he escaped from prison, twice, and walked from Vichy, France across the Pyrenees. I knew my uncle well and was raised as his literal neighbor, yet these and other stories came as a surprise. And throughout the oral passing-on that constituted our remembrance I found myself wishing, time after time, that he—or I—had written it down. A family's history has much to do with just such stories, and I felt a kind of quasi-professional shame at not having told them yet.

So I remember Wallace Stegner the last time we met. He came to the University of Michigan to deliver a series of lectures (on water management, as it happens), and we spent time together. I was complaining in my midlife way about how getting and spending we lay waste our days, how hard it is to muster youth's ambition after a certain number of decades and books. I'd had a similar discussion with John Hersey a while earlier, and his answer was the same. They represented as much as said it: "Nonsense, boy, we're all beginners. It's what happens next that counts—and the work you leave behind." What they leave behind are volumes, and those volumes speak.

When I first became a teacher, well-meaning friends seemed worried. They warned me, in effect, that there were only a finite number of words, that I'd use up my available store of language, depleting the resources a writer must draw on in order to do his true work. It turned out that, for me at least, the occupational hazard of teaching is precisely the reverse— a kind of garrulity, a logorrheic flow. So I can now say in a paragraph what used to take a sentence, can speak at some length with a semblance of conviction on a topic of which I know nothing at all—just by turning on the syntax-tap and waiting to see what pours out.

Therefore silence seems the better part of valor, a way of revaluing language and letting the well fill. Some of the great modernists have embraced this proposition and explored that paradox: Samuel Beckett produced a million words about how hard it was to be accurately expressive. Nothing in the work of J. D. Salinger has been more closely considered than his refusal to publish it, and Marcel Duchamp's most sounding statement was his withdrawal from paint.

Fifteen years ago I wrote and published a novel called *Possession*. It was well enough received, was the first of a trilogy, came out in paperback, and then languished in that genteel obscurity to which most books are sooner or later consigned. I think there was a movie with that title—no relation, one of a series of ghost or succubus stories—and more recently there was a bestseller with the same title by the accomplished British author A. S. Byatt. So I wasn't overly surprised to receive a letter from a company in Hollywood asking about the status of the film rights to the book. These letters come from time to time, and I figured they'd gotten the wrong *Possession*; in any case, the letter, when forwarded by my publisher, was already several weeks old. Nonetheless I called.

The man who wrote the letter took the call and sounded pleased to hear from me. "Hey Nicky baby," he said, "we love this book, we *love* it." He hadn't read it yet, but others in the office had, and the reader's report said *legs*. They were talking Tom Hanks. Since the hero of *Possession* is a seventy-six-year-old Vermonter, a man called Judah Sherbrooke who barely leaves his chair, I suggested gently that he'd got the wrong book and author. Tom Hanks—splendid actor though he be—wasn't quite the age or type I had in mind. "No problem," he said; his company was the company that made *Pretty Woman*, and they were talking Julia too. Since Sherbrooke's older sister is pushing eighty and uses a walker and dips rather too often in the elderberry wine, I averred as how Julia Roberts—splendid actress though she be—was perhaps not quite right for the role.

He was persuasive, enthusiastic, insisting he had the right author and book. He talked on and on till finally I said, "Look, what are we talking about?" And he admitted, "Nicky baby, we ain't talking about squat." The previous week they'd had a change of management and he was out of there. He was history, but it had been terrific talking to me; there were cutbacks everywhere, and when he left he was taking the file. The rest is, or ought to be, silence.

Zeus Xenias is the Greek god of strangers, those wanderers who show up at your door and must be made welcome within. Often a deity comes in disguise—in order, as it were, to test the waters, to gauge the quality of generosity in a farm or town. Something of the same pertains to the god Wotan of Norse mythology, and in French the word *hôte* signifies, according to its context, either host or guest. These are but a few examples of the widely held belief that hospitality matters—that, in a world less domesticated than ours, the traveler requires roof and food.

In America, as I write this, countless doorbells are being rung. A thousand strangers present themselves at a thousand doors. It may be to make a delivery, to read a water meter, to present a petition for signing, or to sell magazines. It may be—as in the case, say, of a broken car or a request to use a telephone or bathroom—in real need. But how many house or apartment dwellers, standing at that door, will fling it wide? Imagine: you declare to this stranger, "Please don't tell me why you're here until you've had a chance to catch your breath. Come in, why don't you, and sit down. Here, this is my favorite chair. Is it sufficiently close to the fire? Take off your shoes, please—no, let me help you; my daughter will wash your feet. We were just about to have supper; won't you join us? Eat, drink your fill; take a shower. Then tell me, when you're ready, who your parents are and where you come from and the reason that you're here."

Needless to say, it's not likely. The only time a doorbell rings and the door can be flung instantly open is in situation comedies, where the TV circumstance requires that an entrance be announced. In real life, of course, we're far more likely to engage in *xenophobia*—the fear of strangers that edges up to hatred, the drawn bridge or locked gate. Yet the scenario of openhanded host and guest, of *xenophilia*, is played out time and time again in Homer's *Odyssey*. It mattered to those hill-bound and sea-scattered tribes that the wanderer be made welcome, and that no questions be asked.

Even now in Greece the ritual observance of hospitality continues; one conducts a transaction with coffee or candy; one concludes a transaction with ouzo or raki, and it's the seller who buys. I mean by this that when you rent a car or examine a sweater in Athens, it's part of the bargain that food be included, that you share at least this purchased remnant and traditional reminder of a feast. In the Plaka, a village on the slope of the Acropolis now largely consigned to restaurants, I met a shopkeeper called Stephanos sitting in a patch of sun and reading his newspaper. He sold leather goods—belts, briefcases, duffels, handbags, purses—and it was the end of the season and he was closing things down.

He had a cousin in Grand Rapids (every Greek has cousins in America or, increasingly, in Australia), and this seemed sufficient reason for a drink. We talked about the weather, politicians, the proto-fascist colonels once in power there, the quiddities of tourism, the fiscal-exchange rate, democracy, the football results, a border dispute. Only in conclusion—sitting back, smacking his lips—did he inquire courteously, "So, tell me; why are you here?"

A university town is, by definition, full of more-or-less-educated transients. And it's an educated guess that it will prove pleasant to visit and that some of the visitors stay. These last are called faculty members. My wife and I had dinner last month with dear friends in Ann Arbor, and at that point in the evening when wine lends its spurious clarity to what is befuddled perception, I recognized that she alone of all the people on the porch had been born in America—if, that is, the borough of Manhattan quite qualifies. Her mother's name is quintessentially American in its linked contrarieties: Aurora de la luz Fernandez y Menendez Greenhouse, and there's been the usual melting inside the family pot. . . .

Our host was Polish and his academic subject is, as he calls it, "remedial Babylonian"; he reads tablets that make Gilgamesh seem clarity itself. The Palestinian author Anton Shammas and the Israeli Rachel Persico were of that party also—married to each other in this country, as they could not have been so easily in the shared land of their birth. I myself was born in England, of parents born in Germany, with an Italian name. This is the rule, not the exception, in our mobile time. To be an immigrant or refugee, or simply to have moved somewhere other than our parents' home, is the commonplace condition of the twentieth century. And there's a concomitant impulse to visit the place of one's birth—or that of one's parents' parents—to hunt the taproot in all this rootlessness. Witness those busy companies that promise you a family tree, those gatherings of clans that ratify what's often an illusion of a rooted past.

Some years ago I was in London, visiting relatives. At a

certain point my uncle and I decided to visit the house where
I was born, No. 3 Holne Chase. It was hard by Hampstead
Heath, a brick structure with a circular driveway that I
remember sifting through, pebble by pebble, hunting my
mother's lost ring. There was a coal chute also, and a pile of
coal I used to clamber to the top of, pelting my pal Robert
Elkeles; I was the king of the castle, and he the dirty rascal.
Then we'd change places and *he'd* throw the coal. My uncle
and I wandered around the locked house, full of sentiment
and what I can only call Proustian remembrance: *this* was
the corner where *that* had happened, *there* was the window
I rubbed at to peer through the chill wintry fog. When we
told my aunt that evening that No. 3 Holne Chase was just
as I remembered it, the perfect container of all such memory contained, she looked up, adjusting her glasses, and said,
"What?" I repeated myself. My absent-minded uncle
absently agreed. His wife was less vague, more precise: "But,
silly, you were born at number 6!"

So all that Proustian recall was refracted, a misremem-
bered past. And though it seems funny and just a touch sad
that history should be so subject to revision, I've come to
feel grateful for such inexactness: the gift, as it were, of
invention. We invent ourselves daily, I think. And some
nights on a neighbor's porch we can, if we be fortunate,
engage in an act of collective imagination—this dear dream
of possibility, strangers establishing home.

Heinrich Schliemann, however, located Troy by taking
Homer literally; the German archaeologist read the epic
poem not as a metaphor but as a fact-anchored accounting
of a people, time, and place. He had the means and the tenac-
ity to mount an expedition, uncovering those "topless towers of Ilium" where once they had been toppled to the sand.
Most field research seems powered by some such belief; the
digger has an approximate idea of what's there to be
unearthed. So the act of discovery is a confirmation of what's
been waiting all along to be revealed: Michelangelo described

his sculpture as figures imprisoned in marble, and what he provided with his chisel was merely release.

In our imaginations we do something of the same. We hunt for Robin Hood in Sherwood Forest, Hamlet in the Danish castle Helsingør, Leopold Bloom in Dublin, and his progenitor Odysseus all over the watery map. It's passing strange to see the way those fabled locations endure—to see the sand at Pilos, for instance, and to remember the blind bard's description of Nestor's "sandy Pilos," or to see boulders off the coast of Sicily reputed to be those an enraged Polyphemus flung. Once we know that what we visit is of consequence, we look with widened eyes—and it helps to be told in advance. But the reverse can also be the case; if you don't know what you're looking for, it's not always easy to see.

In the small Peloponnesian seaport of Gytheion, there's little to write home about—a dock for car ferries from Italy and the islands, a skein of second-rate hotels, a clutch of sidewalk restaurants and dispiriting cafés. In season it's a tourist town; off season it's part of the Mani region that battens down its hatches against the wind and rain. There's a high seawall to keep back spray, and—as with so many of the roads in Greece—garbage dumped beneath (and sometimes hanging from) each tree. It's as though a history of offering up entrails to the gods has ratified, somehow, the habit of disposal: toss out your household's leavings since the dogs and neighborhood cats will pick them clean. At a curve in the road there's an outcrop, an unprepossessing little island connected by a causeway to the town. Elena and I walked to its edge: listless surf, a lighthouse with graffiti, thorns and brambles underneath. From the discarded evidence, couples take their pleasure there at night. That afternoon there were luckless fishermen, a caique putt-putting loudly into port, and a few idlers out on motorbikes, spewing fumes.

It was called, in the old days, Kranae. Legend has it that when Paris abducted his beautiful Helen and fled from Sparta to the shore, they shared their first lovemaking in this place. They hid from Menelaos and disported themselves brilliantly, and in appreciation Paris built a temple to Aphrodite, the goddess of love. After the fall of Troy, however, Helen's aggrieved husband razed the temple and erected one to justice and to punishment instead. Now there's a lighthouse, its windows broken, slogans painted at arm's reach. But of a sudden, the moon rose; the caique cut its engine, drifting; a scent of fennel wafted to us; and Gytheion was magicked by the song great Homer sang.

I've reached one of those milestone birthdays when it's no longer possible to call or believe oneself young. The coy jokes about actuarial tables or life begun at forty, for example, fade. Those referents to Jack Benny at his perpetual thirty-nine are themselves an index of increasing age, since a diminishing proportion of the populace has even heard of that comedian. Aging is a common story, and I won't rehearse it here. But one of the things I find myself doing that I didn't dream of doing half my life ago is opening the newspaper to the obituary page.

You can tell a person's predilection by the section of the paper he or she reads first. There are, of course, those dutiful citizens who start on the front page and work their way through to the end. But a newspaper militates against such plodding progress; each article invites you to turn to a far-distant fold. More habitual, it seems, is a glance at the headlines, then a headlong rush to the sports or entertainment or business or automobile or employment section. A contemporary definition of "Renaissance man," I suppose, would describe a person who can study the entire Sunday paper with pleasure and profit—reading accounts of the convention or stock market or baseball or gardening, say, with the same knowledgeable enthusiasm accorded to the travel section and the book review. At any rate, I now routinely turn from the front to the obituary page. This is not, alas, a function of age only; the plague of AIDS has brought down a legion of our brilliant young. But I have reached that time

of life when almost daily—and without exception weekly—
the newspaper brings mortal news.

There are several versions of and degrees of distance from
any such announcement. The deaths that matter to us most
are not those we learn of via a newspaper; we don't need *The
New York Times* to inform us that a loved one or family
member has just passed away. And it's also the case, of
course, that a certain degree of prominence seems prerequi-
site to a column inch and photograph; we may indeed be
measured by the length of our obits. So celebrity in this case
matters, and many mourn the anniversaries of, say, JFK or
Elvis or Marilyn Monroe.

More common is the news of a glancing acquaintance's
death, where it grows clear as newsprint that we will not
meet again. The finality comes as a shock. Recently I read of
an old neighbor's death, and a notice of the death of someone who once owned our present home. This morning I read
of a financier I'd met once or twice long years ago; of a sudden the tilt of his head came clear, his high-pitched intonation, the way he smoked cigars while sitting on the beach.
And yesterday a woman called Bubbles, the wife of a British
media mogul, stared out at me wearing a wig. In the twenty
years since last we'd met she'd acquired a title and four or
five homes; "I married an empire," she's quoted as saying,
but death has its dominion even there. The glittering eyes—
the ancient, dated photographs—stare out at us unseeing.
We never quite believe, when the photographer comes calling, that it's for this we pose.

The college I attended was status conscious, clearly, and the
degrees of academic achievement were closely watched. Not
only could you be graduated *cum laude*, but *magna cum
laude* and then—holiest of holies—*summa cum laude*. To
reach this last, you had to run the gauntlet of an oral exam—
if you were on the cusp, that is, and your teachers grilled
you in order to decide. I had a friend who was very very
good at English and slated for an oral exam; he was much

less good at acting but fancied himself an actor and therefore entered a competition called the Boylston Prize Speaking Contest. His chosen speech was the first three hundred
lines of Milton's *Paradise Lost*. He strutted and ranted and
declaimed the speech, hand on his heart, and was very very
bad and didn't win the Boylston Prize or, for that matter,
place, show, or even receive an honorable mention.

On the appointed day of his orals my friend came quak-
ing to the room where his committee of three sat in judgment; he opened the door and froze. At the head of the table,
as committee chair, sat the redoubtable Howard Mumford
Jones—a teacher famed even at Harvard for his fierce
authority, his wide-ranging erudition, and his intolerant
exacting preciseness. He did not suffer fools gladly and
thought everyone a fool. He asked the first question, not
looking up. "Mr. X, can you provide the scansion, please, of
the first three lines of *Paradise Lost*?"

Now that's a nasty first request—but most serious college students of English literature (particularly if they've
spent the last two weeks in desperate preparation for an
exam) can provide the answer. The poem begins, "Of man's
first Disobedience, and the fruit / of that forbidden tree,
whose mortal taste / Brought death into the world, and all
our woe," etc. So our friend breathed a sigh of relief and got
through it without overmuch woe and was settling down to
answer the tough ones when Howard Mumford Jones, not
bothering to look up, said, "Correct. Can you provide the
first ten lines, please?"

Well, as it happened, he could. But that's a seriously
nasty question and most of us could not. I surely wouldn't
be able—had I not looked it up just now—to report that the
tenth line reads "Rose out of Chaos: Or if Sion hill / Delight
thee more. . . ." But our friend, remember, had just delivered the speech and knew those ten lines and their scansion
cold. At the end of them, Mumford Jones looked up for the
first time, ceased to tap his pencil, and said, "Very good.
Pray continue."

So there *is* a God who watches out for failed public speakers, or who enjoys a joke. Because our hero continued until, at line seventy-five or so, the professor interrupted him and said, "No further questions. That will be all." His junior colleagues broke out in applause; Mr. X received his *summa*, and all manner of thing was well.

I like this story of course, because it puts comic flesh on that skeletal assertion, "The last shall be first." Had X been marginally better at public speaking, the Harvard faculty would have known he knew *Paradise Lost* and would not have asked him to recite it again. Also, and importantly, this story suggests that the benefits of a ruling passion can prove unexpected. There are high and unanticipated rewards in store for those, say, who hone memory or tinker with radio sets or clay or endgame problems in chess. John Fowles in his "Notes on an Unfinished Novel" puts the case succinctly: *Follow the accident, fear the fixed plan*. That's the moral here. What we think we are winning we may not have won; where we construe ourselves a failure we may yet in fact succeed.

Certain Cycladic sculptures, certain very early Greek artifacts, evoke art made earlier still, and in the south of France. Elena and I returned once more to that region of the Dordogne made famous by cave paintings—that hilly and cavernous region where Ligurian man made his home. The most celebrated of these caves is, no doubt, Lascaux. Its accidental discovery on September 12, 1940 by four boys of Montignac has been thoroughly reported on and, of late, commercialized; there are the predictable T-shirts and postcards and statuettes of Cro-Magnon man wielding a paintbrush. Yet because the atmosphere of the cave was thoroughly disrupted by the hordes of tourists trekking through—all that pollen and carbon dioxide and bacteria from shoes and clothing accreting on the walk—the "real" Lascaux was sealed again in 1963. Some twenty years thereafter a version of the original was reproduced a few hundred meters down the hill, as a concrete cave entitled Lascaux II. Though the artists were scrupulous, using ancient techniques and replicating to the millimeter the great original, the place defines itself as secondhand. Tour buses huddle, like the deer and horses painted within, at its base.

This is one paradox of democracy: the more widely available a site, the less special it becomes. Real estate brokers, museum directors, and advertising copywriters all profit from the claim that a "once-in-a-lifetime" opportunity is yours and yours alone. What was authentic once—be it beach or wilderness, atelier or recipe—becomes its own derivative from the moment of discovery and praise. Call something inimitable, and it is mass-produced. Trumpet someone's love of privacy, and you increase his appeal. So Lascaux *Deux* feels like the television version of Lascaux, the postcard of a painting. And one of the unanswered riddles of the place is why the portraits of men and women there should be both so numerous and primitive, why those who drew the animals with such surpassing skill proved so thick-fingered and sketchy when drawing their own tribe. The modern child who represents a cow does so as clumsily or deftly as she draws herself. Yet the cave humans are stick figures, not high art. Was there some taboo on self-examination or simply an absence of mirrors? Did the painter take his band for granted or fear for some reason to be too precise? At what point, roughly speaking, did the sense of self—and most particularly the sense of self as artist—enter in?

The answers have eluded us thus far, and I won't try to propose one. These artisans remain nameless, long ago and in the dark; we can't possibly illuminate their motives or their moods. But Elena and I found another cave, the authentic Grotte de Rouffignac, to which the atmospheric damage was done so long ago that no one seems to mind exposing it to more. It's a place full of graffiti, centuries of names scrawled over centuries of mammoths—deep and cold and forbidding and off the beaten track. There were a handful of us at the mouth of the cave; a young man took us into it by rail. Several kilometers down, when he switched off his flashlight in absolute blackness, I felt once more that rush of wonder: *How was this done?*

They lay on their backs, the painters. They used stone lamps with animal fat. But the rocks are uneven and porous, not malleable wood or canvas, and the pigment would have been quickly applied and equally quickly absorbed. He who outlined the mammoth's tusks could not have seen the painted tail; it would not have been possible, while working, to view the creature steadily and whole. And whether the painter intended this or not—whether these were images of what his people hoped to kill or what they hoped to entice to the valley once more—the images endure. We work, each one of us, in the deep dark with no notion of what lasts.

Judgment

Ford Madox Ford is known today as the author of "the best French novel in the English language," *The Good Soldier*. Much praised, he has been little read. He produced eighty-one books. Ford's devotees—this writer among them—revere his tetralogy of war novels, *Parade's End*, and trilogy of historical novels, *The Fifth Queen*. He composed idiosyncratic books of biography, several splendid volumes of autobiography and travel. He wrote poems, essays, fairy tales, speculative prose. But whatever one makes of Ford's stature as an author, there can be little doubt of his eye and ear as an editor, his standing at the very center of this century's cluster of talent. He served as expert witness to its literary life. As editor, with the possible exception of Ezra Pound—whom Ford also helped and who performed much the same service for poets—he was nonpareil.

The first issue of his magazine, *The English Review*, appeared in December 1908. It contained a W. H. Hudson essay on Stonehenge and the first installment of Joseph Conrad's memoirs. It offered an installment of H. G. Wells's *Tono-Bungay* and a Constance Garnett translation of Tolstoi. Shorter fiction included a story by Henry James, "The Jolly Corner," and "A Fisher of Men" by John Galsworthy. Ford's taste astonishes; his judgment was fully first rate. This was no proleptic *Norton Anthology*, a selection of agreed-upon survivors, but rather an assessment made in the hurly-burly of the period itself.

And when someone asked him how he managed to read as well as write so much, the novelist made memorable answer. He spoke with difficulty; he had been mustard-gassed in the First World War. A great walrus of a man by then, he wheezed out his description of the role of editor (I have it from the questioner): "It's easy," Ford averred. "It only takes a line."

Some called him a liar; all agree he took a lover's license with truth. He embroidered; he worked for effect. He liked to call himself, after Basho, "an old man mad about writing," and at times his pursuit of narrative could undermine mere fact. So it probably took him a paragraph to decide what to take or reject. But I want to start this essay with an extract from Ford's memoir on discovery—and the process of judgment itself.

> In the year when my eyes first fell on words written by Norman Douglas, G. H. Tomlinson, Wyndham Lewis, Ezra Pound and others . . . upon a day I received a letter from a young schoolteacher in Nottingham. I can still see the handwriting—as if drawn with sepia rather than written in ink, on grey-blue notepaper. It said that the writer knew a young man who wrote, as she thought, admirably but was too shy to send his work to editors. Would I care to see some of his writing?
>
> In that way I came to read the first words of a new author:

"The small locomotive engine, Number 4, came clanking, stumbling down from Selston with seven full waggons. It appeared round the corner with loud threats of speed, but the colt that it startled from among the gorse which still flickered indistinctly in the raw afternoon, outdistanced it in a canter. A woman walking up the railway line to Under-wood, held her basket aside and watched the footplate of the engine advancing."

I was reading in the twilight in the long eighteenth-century room that was at once the office of *The English Review* and my drawing room. My eyes were tired; I had been reading all day so I did not go any further with the story. It was called "Odour of Chrysanthemums." I laid it in the basket for accepted manuscripts. My secretary looked up and said:

"You've got another genius?"

I answered, "It's a big one this time," and went upstairs to dress. . . .

(Ford then proceeds to analyze the first paragraph of D. H. Lawrence's first published story. His reading strikes me as a paradigm of judgment, and worth reproducing at length.)

The very title makes an impact on the mind. You get at once the knowledge that this is not, whatever else it may turn out, either a frivolous or even a gay, springtime story. Chrysanthemums are not only flowers of the autumn: they are the autumn itself. And the presumption is that the author is observant. The majority of people do not even know that chrysanthemums have an odour. I have had it flatly denied to me that they have. . . .

Titles as a rule do not matter much. Very good authors break down when it comes to the effort of choosing a title. But one like "Odour of Chrysanthemums" is at once a challenge and an indication. The author seems to say: Take it or leave it. You know at once that you are not going to read a comic story about someone's butler's omniscience. The man who sent you this has, then, character, the courage of his convictions, a power of observation. All these presumptions flit through your mind. At once you read:

"The small locomotive engine, Number 4, came clanking, stumbling down from Selston," and at once you know that this fellow with the power of observation is going to write of whatever he writes about from the inside. The "Number 4" shows that. He will be the sort of fellow who knows that for the sort of people who work about engines, engines have a sort of individuality. He had to give the engine the personality of a number . . . "With seven full waggons." . . . The "seven" is good. The ordinary careless writer would say, "some small waggons." This man knows what he wants. He sees the scene of his story exactly. He has an authoritative mind.

"It appeared round the corner with loud threats of speed." . . . Good writing; slightly, but not too arresting. . . . "But the colt that it startled from among the gorse . . . outdistanced it at a canter." Good again. This fellow does not "state." He doesn't say, "It was coming slowly," or—what would have been a little better—"at seven miles an hour." Because even "seven miles an hour" means nothing definite for the untrained mind. It might mean something for a trainer of pedestrian racers. The imaginative writer writes for all humanity; he does not limit his desired readers to specialists. . . . But anyone knows that an engine that makes a great deal of noise and yet cannot overtake a colt at a canter must be a ludicrously ineffective machine. We know then that this fellow knows his job.

"The gorse still flickered indistinctly in the raw afternoon." . . . Good, too, distinctly good. This is the just-sufficient observation of nature that gives you, in a single phrase, landscape, time of day, weather, season. It is a raw afternoon in autumn in a rather accented countryside. The engine would not come round a bend if there were not some obstacle to a straight course—a water-course, a chain of hills. Hills, probably, because gorse grows on dry, broken-up waste country. They won't also be mountains or anything spectacular or the writer would have mentioned them. It is, then, just "country."

Your mind does all this for you without any ratiocination on your part. You are not, I mean, purposedly sleuthing. The engine and the trucks are there, with the white smoke blowing away over hummocks of gorse. Yet there has been practically none of the tiresome thing called descriptive nature,

of which the English writer is as a rule so lugubriously lavish. . . . And then the woman comes in, carrying her basket.
That indicates her status in life. She does not belong to the
comfortable classes. Nor, since the engine is small, with
trucks on a dud line, will the story be one of the Kipling-
engineering type, with gleaming rails, and gadgets, and the
smell of oil warmed by the bearings, and all the other tire-
someness.

You are, then, for as long as the story lasts, to be in one of
those untidy, unfinished landscapes where locomotives wander innocuously amongst women with baskets. That is to say,
you are going to learn how what we used to call "the other
half"—though we might as well have said, the other ninety-
nine hundredths—lives. And if you are an editor and that is
what you are after, you know that you have got what you
want and you can pitch the story straight away into your
wicker tray with the few accepted manuscripts and go on to
some other occupation. . . . Because this man knows. He
knows how to open a story with a sentence of the right
cadence for holding the attention. He knows how to construct a paragraph. He knows the life he is writing about in a
landscape just sufficiently constructed with a casual word
here and there. You can trust him for the rest. (From the
Bodley Head Ford Madox Ford, vol. 5).

As indicated above, I revere Ford just this side of idolatry.
The passage demonstrates his informed and alert response,
his gift of split-second discernment. It's an articulated version of the process we engage in every day—the decision to
start a story, finish an article, buy the book. Except in our
role as teacher or friend, we enter into no contract to read—
to fully read—a text; such judgment calls are continual and
quasi-automatic. The IN tray, the OUT tray are with us wherever we go. And as anyone who has engaged in the process
professionally can attest, the OUT tray is much the more full.

Recently, however, I've come to question Ford. First of all,
and though the memoir may be accurate, I have no doubt he
finished the piece later on. He would have saved it out for
closer reading, might have shown it to his second-in-com-

mand. Had Lawrence not been printed in *The English Review*, he would no doubt have found another sponsor soon or late. And the first paragraph may well be the most successful of "Odour of Chrysanthemums"; what follows is Lawrence the tub thumper, the preacher.

Any such judgment, no matter how it purports to objectivity, cannot be absolute. It is subject to caprice. (The reader's eyes grow tired; he looks forward to dinner; the daily fare has been lean.) On that threshing floor for winnowed chaff, the next shift's custodian may pick out grain; after the judgment chamber, there comes a court of appeal. It is a piece of extraordinary arrogance, after all, to decide on the basis of a single line: thumbs up or down. And any set of judges will likely disagree.

The house of fiction has, as Henry James informed us, many rooms. The novel is as changeable a genre as can plausibly be labeled by a single name; so too is the short story. Convention, merely, or laziness of language causes us to classify the work of Jane Austen and William Burroughs in a common category; so too with the brief fictions of Chekhov and Davenport. This may prove the labeler's despair, but it is the reader's delight.

That art is descriptive is clear; that it is prescriptive is to be desired; that it should be proscriptive strikes me as inane. Dangerous too, since that way lies censorship. The virtue of the marketplace lies in its competitive jumble, its contradictory standards, its multiplicity of wares. So how do we go about choosing—in the forum of the classroom or the conference, the office of Simon & Schuster or the drawing room that doubled as the editorial boardroom of Ford's magazine?

De gustibus non est disputandum is a dictum accepted by all. There is no arguing—or at least no instructive disagreement—as to taste. Yet all of us, it seems to me, who spend our lives as teachers—as writers surely also—attempt to ensure the reverse. We have, however unverifiable, our own sense of gossamer truth, our conviction that *this* matters, *that* does not. We have, however hazily conceived or haphazardly constructed, our sense of value, achievement, of what is worth celebration and what not. Few hierarchical systems are more of a muddle than that of aesthetics; how explain why *Moby-Dick* is a better book than *Jaws*? As judges—whether anointed or self-appointed—we are constantly adjudicating this very question: rank.

The term itself is its own oxymoron. "Rank" suggests both the condition of hierarchy, the level of attainment, and its rancid concomitant, decay. "Oh my offense is rank," says Shakespeare's Claudius, implying both at once. "Judgment" too is a word full of shadings—a word as impartial as the ideal practitioner thereof. The Last Judgment, for instance, conveys the threat of failure as well as the possibility of eternal success; "Judge not, lest ye be judged." Think of Augustine's great conundrum: "Do not despair; one of the thieves was saved. Do not presume; one of the thieves was damned."

To be thrown into the "hoosegow" is to have been judged. "I was *juzgado*," the cowboys would say, when south of the border they landed in jail: hoosegowed. Even the judgment of Paris, so happy a circumstance—the first recorded beauty contest—is fraught with peril and freighted with risk; whichever goddess the lucky lover chooses (she daintily taking his hand, accepting the roses, weeping becomingly, smudging her mascara, smiling at the audience, her bosom swelling with emotion, showing the right length of leg while she curtseys) leaves two disgruntled also-rans. And then the Trojan War . . .

Too, our standards of beauty can change. Indeed they should, or we're likely to be accused of arrested development; think of the sixty-year-old who lusts only and repeatedly for the sixteen-year-old's shape. We change our opinions with time. Certain books that meant a great deal to me ten years ago now seem transient, fleeting in appeal; the hallmark of one's youth is not inevitably the benchmark of middle or old age. The very structure of instruction has to do with discernment, with learning how to see what had been hidden before. Think of all those fables where the young man chooses lead, not gold, and discovers the true value of the thing contained; think of those fairy tales where the ancient crone kissed becomes a princess, faithful forever, a boon to the bed. Don't judge a book by its cover, we say, but which of us would truly wish to have a cover so repellent as to forestall judgment or have it predisposed? Nor is the relation of outer to inner always inverse; an ugly cover—lead, the crone—does not guarantee the contents will prove beautiful. Kiss the frog if you so choose, but don't assume it must posthaste transmogrify to prince.

For judgment too shifts locus. It's not as if a single individual has a single standard and bears it aloft throughout a career. Though a writer's work may have a ruling passion and a continuity, though there be two or three governing ideas expressed, nonetheless it's safe to say that a career shifts shape. So blind justice with the scales is an apt metaphor here—as long as we remember that time may tilt the balance, pressing heavy-thumbed and at near-random on a side.

This is a function of variety. It is comparatively easy to judge a tennis match or a diving competition; it's simple enough to determine which piece of pottery is defective, where the violin's varnish has bubbled or the joining cracked. The coincidence of estimates in a gymnast's score-card sometimes makes one feel as if the judges are in league. It's a little less clear in a piano competition, perhaps, or in the submission of blueprints for an architectural project—but here too the parameters have been defined and the standards made available. To the degree that a form has amplitude, however, it grows harder to assess.

I have carried with me for some time—and it is all the more attractive because unclear—the notion of writers as artisans, of artists engaged in a guild. The model is that of the medieval guild, with its compelling triad of apprentice, then journeyman laborer, then master craftsman—this last attained after a lifetime's study and practice of the craft. That writing *is* a craft as well as art, that one must learn to dado the paragraph's joints, as it were, and learn how to prime the scene's canvas—this is something we take increasingly for granted. But the growth from apprentice to master crafts- man seems at least confusing; it is not a mere matter of time. Who provides the walking papers and approbatory judg- ment; who does the training, the teaching; who ratifies our membership and says, "Welcome to the guild?"

There are several plausible candidates. There are agents, editors, publishers; there are critics and prize-giving commit- tees; there are writing programs, hydra-headed lately, and writing conferences and festivals and magazines and an audi- ence of strangers growing intimate as we whisper secrets— with the high hope that thousands will read them—we might hesitate to tell to a close friend. There is inward certainty, discovery: the knowledge that we now can manage what we once could not. There are strange and compelling contests to enter: the lottery called influence, the lottery called fame. But surely one of the ways we know we are writers is when writ- ers tell us so, pointing out a way through the dark wood.

Yeats called it "singing school"—then hastened to insist that none such obtained in Ireland. Not long ago we writers were strangers to academe's grove; now we fit to those grooves like a needle, wearing blunt with usage. And the assumption here, of course, is that practitioners may repre- sent the art with greater precision than critics, since those who teach had better also be those who do. It's a nice dis- tinction, however; we do not assume that a voice teacher need be a better singer than the students he or she may coach; not all managers of baseball teams were baseball heroes earlier; excellence as a writer is not the single meas- ure of those who profess it, who teach.

Antonello da Massina was serving as an apprentice in his master's studio. The commission was nearly complete, the master engaged on his self-portrait in the lower right-hand corner, behind the donor's image—a kind of signature. Then he was bitten by a disease-bearing mosquito and fell ill. From his sickbed he issued the order that the project be completed; from what looked as if it might prove his deathbed, he rose to examine the work. At first sight of the commission he pronounced himself well pleased. Looking more closely, however, at what was no longer a self-portrait in progress but a completed portrait he leaned forward to inspect a black speck on the neck.

"What's this?" he inquired of Antonello. "What is this?"

"Master," said his student, deferential, "that's the mosquito that so nearly killed you."

The painter doffed his cap. "Antonello," he announced, "you're the master now."

The whole impulse toward "self-expression" is a recent and a possibly aberrant one in art. Legions of accomplished writers found nothing shameful in prescribed or proscribed subjects or in eschewing the first-person pronoun. The apprentice in that artist's shop might mix paint for years or learn to dado joints for what must have felt like forever; only slowly and under supervision might he approach the artifact as such.

Nor is "signature" important. The bulk of our literature's triumphs have been collective or anonymous; who can identify the authors of the Bible, the *Ramayana, Beowulf*? More to the point, who cares? The *Iliad* and *Odyssey* are by an unknown bard as are, for all practical purposes, the plays of William Shakespeare. This is not to say that these works don't display personality—the reverse is more nearly true—but rather that the cult of personality should fade. It too is recent and, I think, aberrant; it has nothing to do with the labor of writing as such.

All this conjoins with the nature of language and our presumed literacy—a native familiarity with English that, more often than not in the contemporary author, breeds contempt. No one presumes to give a dance recital without having first mastered the rudiments of dance, to perform Mozart before they've learned scales, or to enter a weight-lifting contest if they've never hoisted weights. Yet because we've been reading since age five, we blithely assume we can read; because we scrawled our signature at six, we glibly aspire to write.

And here, I think, is where the issues of apprenticeship and judgment intersect. Imitation is flattery's form. No first sentence is impossible. The writer is the literal lord of his created domain. (Some first sentences are, admittedly, more possible than others; the reader may choose to stop reading after the opening phrase.) We can point to any world we wish, we make up the rules of our game.

By the second sentence, however, we have fewer possibilities; we begin to follow our own lead. A story that starts from a first-person present-tense vantage would dizzy the reader if it shifted to third person and the past tense on the next page; one that starts in Zambia had better not move to Rhode Island in the second phrase. And if the writer chooses such disjunction, then the third sentence somehow ought to indicate he knows what he is doing—that the story deals with shifting vantage points. For the game we invite a reader to join has a coherent system, and we should not cheat nor alter the rules halfway through.

I do not mean that every story must be linear or that the reader should be able to fathom it by the first paragraph's end. Any situation worth exploring is progressively revealed. But if we understand a woman to be forty we should not learn ten pages later that she's twenty-two; if we're told—authoritatively—X has been a murderer we should not find at story's end that it was really Y. So the process of delimiting continues through the piece; the third sentence follows the second as the second did the first. The thirtieth follows the twenty-ninth, excluding what once might have been. And there should be, ideally, only one last line. Of the infinite range of possibilities with which the writer began he is left with a single legitimate closure—all others having been foreclosed.

This holds true for dialogue as well as for descriptive

prose. If a character's last line must be, "I ain't sure I love you," she can't use the alternative, "Cyril's in dubiety with reference to hate."

So the teacher-judge must first attempt to parse the petitioner's system—to measure, as it were, the distance between intention and execution. Justice is, more often than we care to acknowledge, a matter of interpretation, a "reading" of the law. If you're looking for an adventure story, you won't likely be compelled by *À la Recherche du Temps Perdu*; if you want to read about the contemporary South, you'll be disappointed by *Oliver Twist*. This is self-evident but nonetheless something we tend to forget; each work of original fiction creates and must be measured by its own— always implicit if only rarely explicit—terms. And what we ought to judge therefore is its consonance with such engendered expectation: the degree to which the game's rules have been played.

Ford Madox Ford provided, in the case of D. H. Lawrence, an exemplary instance of judgment. What follows is, I think, a paradigmatic example of the teacher's role. Its strategy insists on imitation, its purpose is to foster originality instead. The speaker is Bernard Greenhouse, one of the founding members of the chamber music ensemble, the Beaux Arts Trio. In the period of which he tells, Greenhouse had already achieved an important concert career. Yet he felt the need to continue his studies—to complete, as it were, apprenticeship. (In my book, *The Beaux Arts Trio: A Portrait*, this story emerges in fragments; I have excised myself as interviewer for the sake of continuity.)

Casals was, as you know, very much occupied with the Spanish Republican cause in 1946. We had a lengthy correspondence, and he refused to teach me. But I did not accept the negative reply. So I took a troop transport right after the war—after I'd come out of the navy. I enrolled in the American School at Fontainebleau as a means to get a visa. And I

took, in addition to my cello, several cases with all sorts of
food which I knew would be in short supply—baking chocolate, tinned butter, that sort of thing. After I arrived in Paris,
I wrote another, final postcard asking whether he wouldn't
hear me play just once. And I received a card in Paris, saying
if I came on such and such a date, he would be pleased to
hear me play—providing I would give a check to the Spanish
Republican charities. When I received the card I was, of
course, overjoyed. I made arrangements to take the train to
Perpignan and then the mountain railway up to Prades. And
I arrived at the railway station speaking barely a word of
French. There was someone with a hand-drawn cart who
took my valise; I carried the cello. We went down the main
street into Prades and to the Grand Hotel. But the owner
shook his finger at me and said—the porter translating—
"No more cellists can come to my hotel. I already had one.
Casals. He disturbed all the guests."

So I had to wend my way over to the midwife's. She happened to have a room free at the time, a room just barely
wide enough for the bed—with no possibility of practicing.
The same day I went to the Villa Colette and knocked on
Casals's door. I was let in. Within minutes Casals came down
from his studio, still in his pajamas; he had been writing letters. And he said, "You have come a long way and been very
persistent. Why have you come here to study with me?" We
sat down, had a long discussion. I gave him my background
and told him some of the works which I had performed; I
said he had been my idol ever since I was ten. He said, "You
go back to your room and come back in two days in the
morning, and I will hear you play."

Well, the next days were anxious ones for me. I went back
on the appointed morning, entered the room, and Casals still
hadn't dressed. He was still in his pajamas. He said, "Well,
now, you warm up a bit, play a bit so that you get your hands
in good condition and I will be back as soon as I have dressed
and shaved." I took the cello out of the case and worked for
twenty minutes or so, and there was no Casals. I had had my
back turned to the door, and when finally I turned I could see
his bald head in the doorway—he had been listening at the
keyhole. When he saw that I had turned my head, he came

into the room, still in his pajamas, still unshaven, and he said, "I really didn't want to dress. I wanted to hear you without having you nervous."

Then he started asking for the repertoire, and he requested many pieces. After an hour or more of my playing—during which he indicated nothing more than the piece and the passage he wanted me to play—he said, "All right. Put down your cello, put it away, and we'll talk." And I thought, now here comes the worthwhile contribution to a Republican charity. But he said to me, "Well, what you need is an apprenticeship to a great artist. I believe in the apprentice system. Stradivarius, Guarnerius, Amati . . . they turned out so many wonderful violin makers. And I believe the same thing can hold true in making musicians. If I knew of a great artist I could send you to, I would do so," he said, "because my mind is occupied with the Spanish Republican cause. But since I don't know whom to send you to—and if you agree to stay in the village and take a lesson at least once every two days—I will teach you."

So I went back to Paris for my trunks, came back and settled in. At this point the gentleman who owned the Grand Hotel—when he found out that I had chocolate and good American dollars—changed his mind about having a cellist in residence. So I moved into the Grand Hotel, had a palatial room with a view, and from that point on I started to work very hard. I had three or four lessons a week.

When I asked Casals how much he would charge a lesson, he said twenty dollars. In those days such a sum was considerable. But one day I arrived in great spirits and I played a beautiful performance—forgive me, I think it *was* beautiful—of the Brahms F Major Sonata. And when I finished he said, "You know, you played so well today I won't accept the twenty dollars." And I was deliriously happy. But the next lesson, unfortunately, I didn't play so well, and he accepted the twenty dollars. This went on until finally he said to me, "You know, I can't accept this money from you, I know it's going to be difficult. But someday when you're able to, I would like you to write a check for the Spanish Republican charities and make a considerable contribution." And this is a promise I've kept.

We spent at least three hours a lesson. The first hour was performance; the next hour entailed discussion of musical techniques; and the third hour he reminisced about his own career. During the first hour, he sat about a yard away. He would play a phrase and have me repeat it. And if the bowing and the fingering weren't exactly the same as his, and the emphasis on the top of the phrase was not the same, he would stop me and say, "No, no. Do it this way." And this went on for quite a few lessons. I was studying the Bach D Minor Suite and he demanded that I become an absolute copy. At one point I did very gingerly suggest that I would only turn out to be a poor copy of Pablo Casals, and he said to me, "Don't worry about that. Because I'm seventy years old, and I will be gone soon, and people won't remember my playing but they will hear yours." It turned out of course that he lived till the ripe old age of ninety-seven.

But that was his way of teaching. He was very insistent about it—extremely meticulous about my following all the details of his performance. And after several weeks of working on that one suite of Bach's, finally, the two of us could sit down and perform and play all the same fingerings and bowings and all of the phrasings alike. And I really had become a copy of the Master. It was as if the room had stereophonic sound—two cellos producing at once. And at that point, when I had been able to accomplish this, he said to me, "Fine. Now just sit. Put your cello down and listen to the D Minor Suite." And he played through the piece and changed *every* bowing and *every* fingering and *every* phrasing and all the emphasis within the phrase. I sat there, absolutely with my mouth open, listening to a performance, which was heavenly—absolutely beautiful. And when he finished he turned to me with a broad grin on his face, and he said, "Now you've learned how to improvise in Bach. From now on you study Bach this way."

Let me finish, therefore, with a set of seeming paradoxes. We must listen with respectful deference to the verdict of the judge—whether it be praise, dispraise, or the most likely, a suspended sentence—and then appeal. We need to know a colon from a semicolon to know freedom within limits as the root and force of syntax. We must work through derivation toward the original voice—remembering that "originality" is likely to be a compound of influences so multiform and various it cannot be defined. Our certainties will turn to doubt, our rote learning grow improvisational.

Remember that the poet, lost in the dark wood, had the great good luck—in the middle of his journey, in the middle of the road of this life—to find another poet pointing out the way. But remember also that the story of instruction, of Virgil's guiding hand, comes to us from Dante's point of view. Look for the fly, if not in the ointment, on the teacher's neck.

Rumford

HIS BOOK

I have been engaged, more or less incessantly, for the last several years on what has been a new departure in my work. It is my self-involved but unabashed intention to discuss that departure, in the hope it might prove instructive; the pratfalls one author has taken may be useful to others who chart the terrain. I'll act, in effect, as point-man in the minefield of historical fiction—describing the beauties of the prospect, and a possible way through it as well as where it may implode.

The professional writer requires, sooner or later, some access to material not constituted from the matter of his or her own life. Once we've used up the small store of our experience (a first novel about childhood, a second about adolescence, a third about young love, then marriage, then divorce) it devolves upon us—or we risk the monotony of repetition—to find something new to discuss.

Some authors manage to make repetition a virtue, to hone and refine their subject and style. They mark out terrain and cultivate it intensively; they compose, of their particular music, variations on a theme. Often (and this is true of music also; think of all those lyrics where the poor benighted singer bemoans his outcast state; he's wand'ring lonely in a crowd or private plane and writing it all down) we make a subject out of a career. Still others—too few of us, admittedly—embrace a seemly silence until we have something to say. In my own case I came rapidly enough off the starting blocks; I published my first novel when I was twenty-three years old and had published ten of them some fifteen years thereafter.

And then the well went dry. While hoping it might fill again, I occupied myself: three volumes of nonfiction and two of short stories have been added to the shelf. But for the last ten years or so I've known, or thought I did, that I was mostly marking time and waiting for a subject larger than its author to appear. My previous two titles, a collection of short stories called *The Writers' Trade* and a nonfiction travel-text-cum memoir called *Running in Place: Scenes from the South of France*, were not, I think, about matters larger or other than their author; they were subjective and inward-facing work. I don't mean to denigrate so much as to describe them; these were books that drew upon lived life and required little research to produce.

A general drift of the novel in our time has been toward self-consciousness. By "our time" I mean this century; by "self-consciousness" I mean the instructed awareness of tradition, and one's relation thereto. As a genre the novel is relatively new, its conventions recent. When Cervantes or Fielding or Stendhal sat down to tell a story they could do so unimpeded—comparatively speaking—by a sense of how their predecessors worked. The wide world furnished topics, and they might range freely. No writer of the nineteenth century would hesitate for long before he made his hero a lawyer, a doctor, an explorer, soldier, scientist, or cleric; to do so nowadays gives many a novelist pause.

This is in part a function of research. The language of doctors and lawyers sounds more specialized to our ears than it did to George Eliot's; the data we require for a convincing portrait of an atomic physicist might even have halted Balzac. The princes and captains of whom Sei Shonagon or Conrad could write have become the property of the mass-market author and therefore doubly damned. One signal of the way our age has increased in specialization is the self-reflexive novel; in theory as in practice now we tend to offer primacy to the world within the word.

So the young man and woman of sensibility take stage center in our books. Often they are sickly or of independent means; often, in pursuit of some spiritual imperative, they hold no daily job. And when they work it's likely, in fact, to be at "the writer's trade." This is a rule to which there are salient exceptions, but it nonetheless applies: more books have been produced of late with the novelist as hero than ever before. Of what else may the writer write authoritatively; what other way of working may we comprehend?

Yet the chance to skirt those boundaries, to enlarge a life's perimeter or—to return to my first trope—to navigate successfully the minefield of the self was one I hoped to take. The advice we give beginning authors is, earnestly, some variant of "Write about what you know." I was, if nothing else, no longer a beginner, and what I knew grew wearisome and what I wanted most of all was to write about some something that I didn't know.

The field was large. But by one of those concatenations of events that some call coincidence and others fate, I stumbled on a subject that declared itself insistently, then would not go away. Some twenty years ago I owned a farm with several fireplaces, one of them formal and shallow and tall. I couldn't make it work, although it clearly had before; it smoked and sputtered out. I gave it up, left it alone, till one of Rumford's adepts appeared and said, "Count Rumford.

It's a *Rumford* fireplace," and showed me how to use it, to stand the kindling up and set the logs upright. Hey, presto, everything was heat!

Then ten years passed, fifteen. . . . A friend of mine is a physicist whose speciality is heat transfer and he told me he was working on the theories of Benjamin Thompson, Count Rumford. The name rang a dull bell; it signified, dimly, that smoke-charged then splendid fireplace, and I asked my friend to tell me, in twenty-five words or more, what interested him about the man and, importantly, the mind. He did so, speaking of heat transfer and Thompson's proof—while working on the Emperor's Arsenal in Munich—that there was no such thing as the previously accepted notion of phlogiston, that heat was not a substance in and of itself. He spoke of Thompson's contribution to practical science, to the dissemination of knowledge and machinery, and of his work as a soldier and spy. Then he mentioned the man's private life; the word he used was "rogue" or "scamp" or "wag." So, by the second bourbon, I was hooked.

Benjamin Thompson was born in Woburn, Massachusetts in 1753. He died as Count Rumford, on the outskirts of Paris, in 1814. His titles would come to include Knight of the Orders of the White Eagle and St. Stanislaus, Privy Counselor of State and Lieutenant-General in the Service of His Most Serene Highness the Elector Palatine, Reigning Duke of Bavaria. He acted as one of General Gage's informers, a loyalist and royalist in "the revolt of the colonies"; he was a founder of the Royal Institution of Great Britain and, it has been argued, the father of nuclear physics. As Sir Benjamin Thompson of London, he was famous for his stoves and experiments in heat and light and coffee pots and mistresses and soups. He loved extravagant clothing and outsize carriage wheels. From a farm boy with a penchant for the grandiose, he became an authentic grandee. The journeys undertaken and the acts of self-transformation were remarkable, as was the man; I undertook to write the novel of his life.

His first marriage was contracted well above his station—to the richest widow in Concord, New Hampshire, where he went as a tutor at nineteen. (The town of Concord had been Rumford, Massachusetts when first settled. Once the border dispute was resolved, however, the banks of the Merrimac River served as boundary between the colonies; the town was renamed "Concord" in honor of that treaty. When he became a Count of the Holy Roman Empire, therefore, Thompson signaled his nobility by taking his wife's town's name.) She was in her thirties and, by his account, rapacious; "She married me, not I her."

Of their brief union, before he had to flee America as a British spy, came Thompson's one legitimate child. Daughter Sarah would not marry, although she wanted to; he sent for her to come to Europe to serve as his companion. Their relationship proved uneasy, often strained; after his death she returned to Concord and hung portraits of his mistresses on the parlor walls. She burned her father's "scolding" letters, and the treatise with which he occupied himself in his retreat in Auteuil. An essay on "The Nature and Effects of Order," it was Rumford's magnum opus—or so he in his correspondence claimed.

In those final years he became more and more a recluse: jealous of his reputation, quick to pick a quarrel when honor was impugned. His second marriage—to the widow of the chemist Lavoisier—proved a spectacular débacle, and he died under a kind of house arrest in Napoleon's France. He busied himself playing billiards and chess—solo, complaining of a "fire" in his head. His final consort and housekeeper was Victoire Lefevre, with whom he had his final illegitimate child.

The career was rich and strange; it resists brief summary. Thompson's published writings run to several thousand pages; his preserved letters are numerous also, as are contemporary accounts. World-famous in his lifetime, he has been almost wholly forgotten. Franklin Roosevelt called him, along with Benjamin Franklin and Thomas Jefferson, one of the three most remarkable minds America produced. He was the single American to be painted by Thomas Gainsborough; his face adorns the Rumford medal conferred by Harvard College; his statue stands at the entrance to the English Gardens in Munich—a park he single-handedly designed. He invented the convertible sofa and the drip coffee pot. He understood the value of wide wheels and double-glazing in windows; his measurement of candlepower remains the standard unit, and he organized the poor and taught them to spin wool. He saved the city of Munich from Austrian and French invasion; his mistress at that period was mistress of the Emperor as well. He became the subject of respectful and satiric rhyme, hagiography and scorn.

But his reputation now stands in near-total eclipse; his experiments with gunpowder, his invention of the "Rumford stove and roaster," his fervent sponsorship of the potato in Europe: these are oddities. A peculiar blend of the eighteenth and the nineteenth centuries—the enlightened and the romantic spirit—informs his life and work. He was vainglorious in the extreme yet took out no patents and wanted no payment for his inventions; a self-made man and social climber, he upheld established order with real zeal. He loved to live near royalty and gloried in their favor, yet his labors were unceasing for "improvement" of the poor.

I referred above to "stumbling" on this subject, to coincidence and fate. Yet that's a notion that bears slightly closer watching—since often enough we stumble on subjects that fail to ignite our interest or fan a small spark into flame. The world is full of instances, of stimuli; the question is—more properly—what causes our response?

Here we venture on uncertain ground: the kind of answer it's tempting to fabricate after the fact. Benjamin Thompson was born in America, moved early on to England, made his fortune in Bavaria, and died as an exile in France. These are the four countries to which I can connect. I myself was born in England, of parents born in Germany, and make my home if not fortune in America, and have lived in France. More important, there plays about Thompson's career the issue of rootlessness, restlessness, and the image of a self-invented wanderer who likes to think himself empowered by intelligence to rise above mere nationality: a creature, then a noble, of the world.

In this he proved deluded: he died sick and embittered, alone. His name was writ in water though he thought it hewed in stone. His maiden daughter, dying, left his considerable estate to two charities: a home for parentless children and the New Hampshire Asylum for the Indigent Insane.

It should be evident by now that the language I deploy to describe our hero has a certain rhetorical formality to it—and this also played a part in the process of choice. It was easier for this particular writer to acquire and then ape the discourse of eighteenth-century Europe than it would have been to fake the street slang, say, of twentieth-century Detroit. Further, and with reference to research, it gave me genuine pleasure to read the "Essays" of Count Rumford (those musty tomes once unearthed) with something like comprehension of the matters he discussed. I couldn't hope to understand the workings of contemporary physics, but his straightforward arithmetic proved manageable. I could, or so I told myself, make sense of this career. He was in fact a scoundrel and a sexual adventurer—a rogue, a rake, a wag, a mountebank, an *arriviste* and *parvenu*—and all of that helped too.

The house where he was born in Woburn still stands. I went to see it, went to see the garden he designed in Munich, went to see the Royal Institution in London in upper Albemarle Street. When you start looking for something, it crops up everywhere. There's a Rumford Roaster in Henry Ford's Museum; there are recipes for soup that bear his name. There's a baking soda and a book about old stoves that someone found and sent me, celebrating Rumford; there's that astonishing Gainsborough portrait of Thompson in the Fogg. So I found myself, it's fair to say, invaded: regaling friends at dinner, buttonholing physicists, haunted by the wreckage of the life. One *can* become thus haunted, thus invaded—talking to oneself in the accent of a character, embracing attitudes not one's own. It's one of the strange yields of composition that, sitting at a desk in modern dress and using a word processor, one can almost literally be transported to nineteenth-century Munich under siege or argue with patriots in eighteenth-century Salem or watch a Parisian coquette disrobe in the candlelit dark. . . .

I have wandered far afield from the general subject: history as fiction, a fictive history. (It might be worth mentioning, parenthetically, that much of what we construe to be the world's great literature—the *Iliad*, the *Aeneid*, *The Tale of Genji*, *Henry V*, etc.—replicates a history long past. One need not be eyewitness to an era or event in order to imagine it persuasively in language; Stephen Crane's vivid war book is based on battles that antedate his birth, and Fabrizio in *The Charterhouse of Parma* watches the Battle of Waterloo from the engulfing mud. Every present action will be someone else's history, and distance may prove useful in the space-time continuum; we have no way of knowing if the bard who gave us Beowulf was present at the table when Grendel came to dine.) In this present age, however, there are three ways of writing historical fiction that seem to me germane.

The first, and the least interesting as well as the most popular, is that version of history that borrows names and costumes, and clothes itself in the regalia of a collective memory. This is the sort of book that re-creates the death of Christ or the birth of Abraham Lincoln or the love affair of Empress Catherine's lady-in-waiting with Rasputin, and does so with no attempt at verisimilitude in language or period style. The details may be accurate; in fact they're quite likely to be. Anachrony is to be avoided, and though the research may be scrupulous the psychological enterprise is, for all practical purposes, sham. It's a kind of bodice-ripper, in which the heroine is always fetchingly in deshabille and the hero is always handsome and the toilets always flush. The villain may not have horns or claws for hands or fins for feet, but he's a constant double-dyed villain who must repent or fail to at tale's end. These are books about King Arthur or Piltdown Man and his pet bear or forward-facing history: sci-fi. If you think of science fiction as a kind of historical novel you'll see, perhaps, what I mean: the details of the enterprise are often ingenious and usually inventive, but the fancy dress of it cannot disguise the recognizable forked animal beneath—the robot with the heart of gold or extra-terrestrial thug.

Second, and more artistically ambitious, is a present reconsideration of the past. I have in mind those books that re-create a history but tell you that they're doing so—that focus, as it were, through microscope or telescope, then proudly display the machine. In this subset of the historical novel the writer may seem to embrace Joyce's notion of a dramatist—"outside, indifferent, paring his fingernails"— but soon or late he'll step stage center and take a curtain call; he'll tell you that the whole of it was fond illusion, sleight-of-hand, and show you what he carries up his sleeve.

Consider Charles Johnson's *The Middle Passage*, in which the enslaved nineteenth-century narrator, Rutherford, spouts Aristotle persuasively and conjures Disney World. Or think of John Fowles's *The French Lieutenant's Woman* or John Barth's *The Sot-Weed Factor* or Julian Barnes's *Flaubert's Parrot* or A. S. Byatt's *Possession*—the list is engagingly long. These are ruminations, as it were, engendered by a history and profiting therefrom for drama—but nonetheless and ostentatiously contemporary texts. They use the past as a kind of vanishing point in order to triangulate the present moment and to establish perspective. It helps if it's a darn good yarn, a rollicking entertainment, and often these stories are at least in part comedic; laughter is loudest when collective and we all are invited to share the joke.

Then finally there's that strange hybrid, the marriage of convenience between style and substance, what the French call *forme et fond*. It's a kind of inflection from context, a viral transmission, infection by data: a way of being so wholly absorbed by matter that manner follows suit. I think here of Mary Lee Settle's Beulah Quintet, of Ford Madox Ford's *The Fifth Queen* trilogy, of Patrick O'Brian's Aubrey and Maturin novels or George Garrett's contemporary foray into Elizabethan England—*Death of the Fox, The Succession,* and *Entered from the Sun.* Or—just to list recent recipients of the Booker Prize—Barry Unsworth's *Sacred Hunger,* Michael Ondaatje's *The English Patient,* and Pat Barker's trilogy *The Ghost Road.* As we approach the millennium there are retrospects as well as prospects, at least as many backward- as forward-looking texts.

These are not so much re-creations as inventions of a language. They might not persuade historians of perfect authenticity in detail and discourse, but they enter imaginatively into and thereby make—remake—a world. They are in a real sense my models, my masters, and they gave me tongue-tied entry to the singing school.

Let me give a sample, or example, of the problem posed. Here is the opening page and a half of *Rumford: His Book*—the first beat. It is representative of the story soon to follow, and it's self-contained. The passage serves as prologue and is dated 1814:

> They laughed at him. They watched him pass. Mothers drew their sons to the embrasure of the window and, peering, pointed him out. "Formidable," they whispered. "Extraordinary. It is something to remember and tell your children's children you have seen. Look!"
>
> Around the corner, rattlingly, the Count appeared. Along the Avenue des Ternes and stopping to collect his glass beyond the Place des Ternes—around the corner, well concealed, not in the industrial center but from their spies dis-

guised—the beakers and alembics privately prepared for him, the necks in their tight spirals blown according to his secret and exact specifications, these coded in his assistant's German so that the envious incompetent calumniating French could not copy and then take the credit—from Boulevard du Bois le Prêtre, along the Avenue de Clichy and out at its high gate; from Malesherbes, Courcelles, along the Boulevard des Batignolles, or to the north—Berthier, Bessières— he made his great processional: one coach.

The women stared. They smiled. They cradled their young sons and kissed them on the cheeks. "You must not forget this, darling, what you see." And little Jean or Claude or Michel or Philippe would approach the window, greatly daring, and promise to remember and press a cold nose to the glass.

They called their daughters also. "Come and watch this. Remember," they said. The worldly ones—the eligible— gazed boldly down at his carriage; the modest averted their eyes. No window was unoccupied, no doorway empty where he went. Old women peered through the drapes. Old men muttered sagely or shook their powdered heads. Servants caught a glimpse, or tried to, crowding near the gate. They jostled for position by the garden wall. The brazen ones braved passage in the street.

There his horses thundered: four white stallions draped in white. Their braided manes and upright tails were clipped. They did not require blinders. Their nostrils plumed; their hooves struck sparks from the cobblestone, clattering: rapid, stately, matched. The coach doors bore his crest. His wheels were thrice the width of wheels on any other équipage, the felloes broad and stable. Careening round the corner, his carriage did not lean.

The Count wore white. It is seemlier in winter, he maintained; it reflects the sun's irradiating heat. From head to toe, from cap to boot and cape to glove he clothed himself entirely in white.

Wherever mad brilliant famous ancient Count Rumford went that season was a sensation: all Paris observed him; all gaped. He moved as if impervious through clamor and derision and applause and whistling fuss. At times he doffed his cap. He tightened the fur at his neck. For what was extraordinary to the populace was, to the object of their wonder, simplicity itself. He smiled and waved and bowed from the waist. Or he paid *la foule* no notice and drove on.

A brief foray into that perilous terrain—the explication of one's own text—should here suffice. I wanted to establish, early on, that my hero was a person of some consequence: people paid attention to him and therefore, by extension, the reader ought to do the same. Soon enough we begin with his childhood, and the rest of the novel works up. But I thought it useful to presage the end—if only to arouse a small-scale tension between the grandee in the coach and the farm boy we'll meet next.

The first word uttered is "Formidable." The reader will perhaps respond to this as a French word—*Formidable*—and a somewhat arch attempt to argue that the language spoken in the street is foreign, not our present English. So too with the last sentence; *la foule* is the French term for "mob." At any rate I wanted those words, "Formidable. Extraordinary," to suggest a kind of formality in diction that would distance us in time as well as space. Then I traced the Count's route and listed a batch of street names, which posed the first real problem. I've been to Paris and know it a little, but the events of Rumford's life took place before Baron Haussmann redesigned the city and redesignated streets. So I obtained a set of maps of Paris in the early nineteenth century, assumed that our hero would arrive from the direction of Auteuil, his home, and traced a grid of streets upon those ancient sheets. The gates of Berthier and Bessières were a bit of an issue, since these were named after Napoleon's marshals, and I couldn't determine what year he named them—but I figured, what the hell, he wasn't in a position to do much naming after 1815, and no one's that likely to notice and anyway it isn't history, it's art.

Then I showed this to a friend who knows Paris well, and he said, wait a second, there aren't and never would have been glassblowers in that *arrondissement*, make him go somewhere else. The second paragraph suggests that the Count had grown suspicious of his hosts—which is true; that he had his glass blown secretly for him so that the French couldn't copy and then take the credit for his inventions, and he employed a German instrument maker to help with the work. Now I happen to know the name of that instrument maker, but it seemed merely showy at this stage to introduce Charles Artaria. And I had grown sufficiently fond of the prose rhythm by that time not to want to change it—which explains the phrase, "around the corner, well concealed, not in the industrial center but from their spies disguised." I figured my friend might be right that there were no glassblowers in the Place des Ternes, but damned if I was going to hunt up another map; I'd make a secret shop.

This principle of, if you will, lazy historicity applies throughout. I know that the Count wore white and invented, for all practical purposes, the wheel. Which is to say that carriages, previously, used thin and wooden wheels; he thickened them for balance on the cobblestones and curves. Hey, presto, our contemporary tire. He also suspended the coach on leather straps, forerunners of our springs. But whether his horses were white, or whether he had four of them, I didn't bother to determine. He's my invention, after all, not the subject of biography (there are two or three on Rumford, mostly focused on his physics) and if I want bold girls to stare and wizened men to cackle, then I'll have them wave and laugh at him while he rattles down the street. It was a risky proposition, a kind of tightrope to walk, and I won't pretend I kept my balance easily or always; I've written a couple of biographies, in fact, and would never dare to do this sort of casual research within that genre instead. Nonetheless it seems to me that the domain of research in historical fiction is strangely delimited: you need to get things right but need to stop your study when imagination starts. It's a kind of starter motor; you turn that particular key until the true engine kicks in.

By now it should be evident that the "true engine" for this author had to do with entry into an alternate system and life. This has marginally to do, I suppose, with some notion of the antiself, an escape from personality into impersonality by opposition, the slackening ego a border increasingly easy to cross. Art does provide that passport and escort over boundaries, that empathetic access to a world otherwise closed. Let me repeat that young Ben Thompson is reported to have said—less than chivalrously—about his first marriage to the wealthy aging widow in Concord, "She married me, not I her." In my book and because I did not write it in first person, the phrase appears as "She married him, not he her." By the alchemy of transposition—a distancing effect with which most writers are intimately familiar—the third person "him" and "he" permitted "me" to enter Thompson's "I."

His second marriage was a catastrophic and very public failure, and it made Paris laugh. He married, again, a rich widow—though by this time he was rich himself and desired not so much her fortune as her fame. She kept a salon in the city; she was the celebrated helpmeet and survivor of the chemist Lavoisier. She liked to entertain; she had friends the Count did not approve of, and she would not change her habits just to conform to his. This is an extract from a letter he sent his daughter Sarah about their contretemps.

Paris, Rue d'Anjou
24th October, 1807

I can do no more, my Dear Sally, than simply give you the anniversary of my marriage, for I am still here, and so far from things getting better they become worse every day. We are more violent and more open, and more public, as

may really be said, in our quarrels. If she does not mind
publicity, for a certainty I shall not. As I write the uncouth
word quarrels, I will give you an idea of one of them. . . . I
am almost afraid to tell you the story, my good child, lest
in future You should not be good; lest what I am about
relating should set you a bad example, make you passionate, and so on. But I had been made very angry. A large
party had been invited I neither liked nor approved of, and
invited for the sole purpose of vexing me. Our house being
the centre of the garden, walled around, with iron gates, I
put on my hat, walked down to the porter's lodge and gave
him orders, on his peril, not to let any one in. Besides, I
took away the keys. Madame went down, and when the
company arrived she talked with them,—she on one side,
they on the other of the high brick wall. After that she
goes and pours boiling water on some of my beautiful
flowers.

What writer could resist such actual written language?
One wants to warble, chorus, descant on the scene. This is
what I made of it—operatic, admittedly, but flat-out fun to
write:

His flowers, his beautiful blossoms! His roses nonpareil! His
dahlias and his violets and brilliant soft anemones and tulips
in a row! How could she trample on his flowerbed, though
trampling on his heart! His amaryllis scalded and his lilies
boiled! Her cloven heels in wanton boots so brutal to his
buds!

The Count was inconsolable; he was wedded to a witch. He
had bound himself with vows and civil contracts and hon-
eyed promises of duty to a fiend. His wife was Jezebel, a har-
ridan, who did him grievous wrong. He—the very definition
of fidelity, of trust and sweet confidingness—compacted with
a slut. He had married sorrow and confusion and implacable
obscenity and a remorseless foe.

He had leisure to reflect on this, and how it came to pass.
Love's melody had turned for him to discord, contrariety and

sheer unlovely noise. How painful to a listening ear, how cacophonous and mournful sounds the instrument unstrung! How bitter and unpalatable tastes the sweet draught staled!

It was no small irony, he knew, that this his second marriage should thus replicate his first. That he who so prized ladies and had been so often prized by them should twice have been so terribly mistaken was a shock. Of all his glad companions—his amours and affairs beyond counting—only these two caused him sorrow; only his wives gave him pain. The widows Rolfe and Lavoisier had this in common: him. What had he done or failed to do to merit such a fate? Whatever he had done, he knew, he did nothing to deserve that pair, a punishment outstripping any crime.

When he reflected on it by himself, he was by himself absolved. So modest a suitor, so amiable a consort had not been found in Paris in these seven years! When he tried to make of their abode a fit and proper place to work, she summoned her old lovers in to play. While he attempted reason, she was illogical in argument and in discourse rude. She screamed and kicked and bit. When he suggested affably that she might moderate her howls, she doubled their volume instead.

So Benjamin Thompson, Count Rumford, went down on his knees by the wall. The iron grating of the fence and brickwork of the gateway, the porte cochère and porter's lodge each signaled his imprisonment, his friendless captive state. His glorious flowers, his darlings, his buds!—she boiled them, one and all.

I began by asserting that this is a minefield, a fearsome terrain, and I want to close with the admission that it may well be booby-trapped in ways I failed to foresee. I'm at that stage of composition where everything has turned to ash, where all the brilliant wit of it sounds stale. That necessary stage, in truth, for all of the best cutting is done when one's sick of the writing, and the pleasure of revision is like pressing on a bruise. . . .

First, this vaunted escape from the self is useful only to

a degree; stray too far in that direction and there's nobody at home. It's possible—probable, even—that such ironical dispassion can be overdone and that the distance intrinsic to historical narration will prove hard to bridge. I mean by this not that we must always identify with all of our creations, and have them face contemporary issues that we've tricked out as timeless, but rather that a certain irreducible affinity must survive the transposition. Otherwise, however impressive, we have a mere period piece. We get beguiled by research, or I did; we get carried away naming names. Whole swatches of information in my novel (the list of subscribers to the Royal Institution, the names of the enlisted men in Thompson's regiment at Henniker, New Hampshire, the dimensions of the carding hall in the Municipal Workhouse at Au) ought still, I suppose, to be cut.

But I became so proud of it, so pleased with myself for having acquired the data that it seemed doubly hard to dismiss. And all those lovely extracts from his essays and his letters—the ring of authenticity that detail can provide—I mourn them in advance. They are superstructure, scaffolding, and have to be removed. The very sort of information a biographer requires may at a given moment come to impede the novelist—yet to recognize impediment is not, for this writer at least, as easy as it sounds. Nor does that recognition necessarily entail its remedy: the lists were such fun to compile. One falls in love with detail; one gets lost in the forest of trees.

There's a concomitant danger, not quite so clear to describe. To spend a year, or three, or five as citizen of a separate world is to become unfamiliar with the world one leaves behind. It's possible Count Rumford is no more than a hobbyhorse and not the gallant stallion I thought I ought to ride. I know the names of the horses he rode—Fawn, then Tancred, then Lambkin—but should perhaps have looked them rather more closely in the fictive mouth. The distance between intention and execution seems cavernous these days; how could I ever have believed I'd manage to incarnate a man who lived two hundred years ago, in four separate countries, and a physicist to boot? My "magnificent obsession," if you will, rings faintly hollow to me even as I describe it, and I sense on my own face the glazed politeness with which for the last years my friends and interlocutors endured this windy enthusiast, this well-intentioned bore. I'm serious, in fact: if tomorrow someone comes to me and says, hey, I have this amazing project, I've discovered this incredible lady, she was a chemist in the sixteenth century and besides she changed her name and lived in Portugal and I'm going to spend the next years learning *everything* about her, I'll nod and smile and think "God help you," and hunt the nearest door.

Telephone

We start with an old joke. Thomas Alva Edison decides to make a telephone. He wants a new invention. He's a whiz with electrical fields, components, the magneto, the disk; he puts all these together and appends a speaking horn. His assistant ventures, "Sir, I believe there's some mistake. You've made a gramophone." "Nonsense, my boy," rasps Edison. "Hush up, I'm expecting a call." After protracted labor, he cranks the machine, puts a needle on the record and, being deaf, does not hear it. Then he puts his ear to the speaker and, listening, says "Hello?"

Innovation. A primary meaning, according to the *Oxford English Dictionary*, is "the alteration of what is established by the introduction of new elements or forms." For the literary imagination, however, a botanical definition of the term comes closer to the mark: "The formation of a new shoot at the apex of a stem or branch; esp. that which takes place at the apex of the thallus or leaf-bearing stem of mosses, the older parts dying off behind; also (with pl.) a new shoot thus formed."

The poet John Clare required his intimate landscape so deeply—the view from the window unchanging—that he went mad when moved. What his father and his grandfather had looked at—"the older parts dying off behind"—delimited his sense of the permissible; what he had not seen before went beyond the pale. Think of those blind weavers with eidetic memory—those who know the way a rug is woven and need not refer to a frame. They may pick up the pattern with no shift of rhythm, without a design established or picture to consult. The innovative artist, however, being what he is, cannot be what he reports on: the scribe is set apart. Much has been written of the sorrow and the privilege of such apartness, the dizzying vistas entailed. What I mean to point to is the inescapability of that separation: how the observer alters each scene and speech observed.

Ronald Blythe, considering Clare, offers this: "I believe that, whether with a feeling of relief or despair—or both—the majority of what are called regional poets and novelists come to a similar decision. Their feeling for nature and the landscape of man deepens when it remains hedged about by familiar considerations. Paradoxically, they discover that it is not by straying far from the headlands that they are able to transport their readers into the farthest realms of the imagination and its truths, but by staying put."

The hunt for voice, for clarity . . . like fiddling with the radio dial, waiting for static to clear. And out of nowhere, suddenly, language emerges. Such a search is likely to remind us of reception, not transmission, waiting for the fuzzy inexact mumble to declare itself. It's a more modern notion, of course, than waiting for "words from the wind." How many can, as did Rilke and Yeats, pace castle parapets? The voices that invade are, often as not, uninvited: the telephone, the television, Muzak, the ghetto blaster on the beach. ("Sir, I believe there's some mistake. You've made a *gramophone*.") But when the work goes well, it does partake of such transmission: in an age of electronics, our version of the vatic voice. News from the Delphic Oracle every night at six.

The risk of forcing one's voice equals the risk of repetition; ventriloquy can prove as wearing as the monotone. The spectacle of academics trying to write like Mickey Spillane is no more edifying than would be the reverse. The writer who keeps shifting ground finds no securer purchase than the one who does not move.

Something seems at best comic about American ancestor worship, the D.A.R. and that newly flourishing mail-order enterprise, the genealogy mill. For twenty-five dollars you too can have a coat of arms; for twenty-five hundred we'll transplant the family bush. Such study is in any case a leisure occupation, the kind of pursuit that the wealthy and retired might embrace. And it smacks, all too often, of fraud.

This, from Malcolm Lowry's *Through the Panama*:

> I am capable of conceiving of a writer today, even intrinsical-ly a first-rate writer who simply cannot understand, and never has been able to understand, what his fellow writers are driving at, and have been driving at, and who has always been too shy to ask. This writer feels this deficiency in himself to the point of anguish. Essentially a humble fellow, he has tried his hardest all his life to understand (though maybe still not hard enough) so that his room is full of *Partisan Reviews*, *Kenyon Reviews*, *Minotaurs*, *Poetry* mags, *Horizons*, even old *Dials*, of whose contents he is able to make out precisely nothing, save where an occasional contribution of his own, years and years ago, rings a faint bell in his mind, a bell that is growing ever fainter, because to tell the truth he can no longer under-

stand his own early work either. . . . At the age of 37, having acquired a spurious fame for various pieces that, as I say, he has long since ceased to understand himself, he wakes up to the fact that he has really only enjoyed with aesthetic detachment four things in his life. A poem by Conrad Aiken, a performance of *Richard II* when he was 10 years old at the Birkenhead Hippodrome, a gramophone record of Frankie Trumbauer's with Eddie Lang, Venuti and Beiderbecke, and a French film directed by Zilke (rhymes with Rilke?) called *The Tragedy of a Duck*. Despite this, he still heroically reads a few pages of William Empson's *Seven Types of Ambiguity* each night before going to sleep, just to keep his hand in, as it were, and to keep up with the times. . . .

Lowry sketches a truth in this portrait. First, that most writers—most autodidacts, perhaps—nurse private fears as to the limits of their learning, suspecting their knowledge to be surface-skitter. Each of us deduces the elephant from tusk, ear, belly, tail. We have eccentric memories, egocentric aspirations, and our handhold on "the great tradition" is reach outstripping grasp. And, further, the knowledge may be skewed. "Because it isn't that this man is not creative, it is because he is so creative that he can't understand anything; for example, he has never been able to follow the plot of even the simplest movie because he is so susceptible to the faintest stimulus of that kind that ten other movies are going on in his head while he is watching it." So my own knowledge of Swedenborg, Blackstone, the politics of Mexico in 1938—not to mention Bunyan, Dante, Blake—derives from close study of *Under the Volcano*: root system inferred from the leaf.

Fiction is a web of lies that attempts to entangle a truth. And autobiography may well be the reverse: data tricked out and rearranged to invent a fictive self. Why should I believe Lord Russell's assertion that he can remember what his mother told him any more than I disbelieve Proust? We've all had the experience of forgotten history, the reinvented past.

Then there's self-engendered history, the slightly tailored tale, the story told so carefully we tell it letter-perfect several times in the same night. The novelist imagines history: his protagonist has a maiden aunt, for instance, and it is her birthday. Therefore we should know where the party takes place, whether she prefers chocolate or carrot cake, if her rejected suitor still wears argyle or striped socks after his operation for cataracts last winter, and what the weather is on August 23rd. So the writer may make something out of nothing and add to the world with no fear of subtraction, feeding her hundred birthday guests on air.

We each create our pasts. I cannot remember the moment when I began to speak and cannot remember the moment at which I decided to write. Rather, and naturally, the whole is a continuum. It is a series of moments and set of lines crossed that appear far clearer in retrospect than they ever did in prospect. To take one such example, I do remember learning how to read. I had just turned six years old and was with my family on the *Queen Elizabeth*, crossing from Southhampton to New York. On the third day of the voyage out—having passed some watermark that meant we were closer to America—I received my first pair of long pants. And that afternoon (sitting cross-legged on the stateroom floor, so proud of my flannels I hated to crease them, the sun through the porthole spotlighting the letters) I taught myself to read.

It was a book about boats. There was a lighthouse, a bridge, a series of ships—from trireme to frigate, canoe to destroyer, with two whole pages devoted to the fireboats, their spray a white, wet arc. The captions distinguished between them; so could I. The alphabet's tumblers went "click." I remember the feel of it, the pride in it, the pleasure, the way the world made sense. I think I remember telling my father I had no time for shuffleboard; I know I took the book up to the deck for tea. It was wonderful—the way the lines pictured this life I was leading. Everything signified; everything fit. Our steward was called Jonathan; I recognized his name badge as his name. The rest of the trip is a jumble, but this sudden perception of order—the deck chairs ranked in rows like language, how a page is organized and why you turn it when— remains indelible. I learned to read that day.

Three years ago, however, I was sorting through some papers in the attic of my father's house. He was moving once again, and I had come to help discard the past's detritus. In a box full of grade-school report cards, letters home from camp, and other such accumulation, I came across a book titled *Henry's Green Wagon*. It was familiar, faintly; it conjured up Great Britain, not the United States. The boy on the disintegrating cover was pink-cheeked and wearing blue shorts. I read the inscription. "To Master Nicky Delbanco," it said. "The best reader in Miss Jamaica's Kindergarten Class. First Prize."

Miss Jamaica's was the school across the street. Like any other English child, I had been taught to read *before* the age of six. So the memory is false. It is clear but confused. Although I remembered the school, the vast-seeming meadow I would traverse on the way home, the hedgehog's lair, the way my aunt would shepherd us, a clearing in the woods that I called Hansel's house—though I remembered much of this, I had forgotten I knew how to read. There are explanations. Probably I learned in stages. Maybe I faked it with *Henry's Green Wagon*, having memorized the book, then turning the pages when it seemed proper to turn. That sunshot moment on the *Queen Elizabeth* may have illuminated something else instead. The transatlantic crossing was a rite of passage, after all, and what I learned while sitting on the deck chair may not have been the alphabet. Therefore the critic's question: how accurate are such accounts?

Think of the difference in Faulkner between the characters who have a past and those who have a future—those obsessed by loss and those who scheme for gain. It is, in effect, the opposition of the Compsons and the Snopeses, the aristocratic and commercial man. In this forward-facing nation—with few exceptions finally—the latter wins. And when, as in Gatsby, the "commercial" man loses, it is because of his instinctive generosity, his aristocratic dream. We are full of nostalgia, the elegiac impulse—but the settler holding up his pitchfork in the face of a bulldozer represents the noble savage, not a feudal lord. To be a "conservative" is to have possessions worth keeping; to be a "survivalist" is to stockpile food and arms. And when we talk of shelter now we mean the tax shelter, not roof.

The burden of the past—Aeneas with Anchises, fleeing Troy. In a way the early author had it easier, had fewer doubts. Since the stuff of the epic was constant, the apprentice could focus on telling; with "matter" taken care of, one learned "manner" as if to it born. Tell the tale of a monkey copulating with banana peels upside down in a space capsule, since it's never been done before. Tell it from the capsule's point of view. It's possible, in other words, that the problem remains one of "what to write," not "how to write it"—and that a great burden of proof would be lifted from the apprentice author if subject matter simply didn't enter in.

My books are, I suppose, importantly concerned with the presence of the past. Characters live at home or hunt it; they know their grandparents or mourn the not knowing; their characteristic motion is digressive, and memory's side-shuffle represents advance. Rootless, they want roots. "All the dead and the mad are in my custody, and I am the nemesis of the would-be-forgotten," as Bellow's Herzog boasts.

But the truth is I'm forgetful, or uninquisitive. My father can cite scores of relatives, their intricate interlocking histories, for each one I absorb. There's a family tree somewhere, and I refer to it pridefully, making sidelong comments about the fifteenth generation, the fifteenth-century Delbancos of Venice, the Palazzo Bernardo they occupied once, their journeys north and west. Yet I know very little of such history and have no desire to ferret it out. Perhaps I fear it will prove, on closer inspection, less grand than I like to assume:

bürgerliche Jews turning away from the ghetto or bustling till buried within. And I can't remember who did what, or when, or moved why where. What's past is prologue—possibly. Yet we are exhorted to face forward, not look back. Has not prolepsis supplanted the flashback as the fashionable device? Cassandra and Tiresias, those early champions of the flash-forward: blind sight.

Tradition as a circus act: the human pyramid. There are strong men at the bottom, with feet on their shoulders, and those who stand upon them holding those who stand. It takes a higher jump, a nimbler weight to vault to the pyramid's top. Up there the balance no doubt feels precarious: the juggler at the apex teeters to applause. Or is it less prepossessing— twelve clowns in a VW who circle the arena, then topple tumbling out? This is what John Barth has called "the literature of exhaustion," or parody as parity (parrotty?), the former dittoing form.

"The day before yesterday, in the woods near Touges, at a charming spot near a spring, I came across some cigar butts and some bits of pâté. There'd been a picnic there! I described exactly that in *Novembre* eleven years ago! Then it was purely imagined, and the other day it was experienced. Everything you invent is true: you can be sure of that. Poetry is a subject as precise as geometry. . . . My poor Bovary is without a doubt suffering and weeping even now in twenty villages of France." So writes Gustave Flaubert, in a letter to Louise Colet, August 14th, 1855. Add to this notion of fiction as fact's prospect the fact of fictive retrospect, and the gift of genuine invention: then Bovary will bring a book to read while he smokes his cigar near the spring. . . .

As a career extends there's the problem—not one the younger writer need consider—of slackening inventiveness. We've said it before, maybe volumes ago, said it as well as we could. The comfort-rounds of habit grow harder and harder to break.

There's nothing wrong with this, no reason each new book need break new ground. Some "formula" writers, indeed, should be wary of change—or their readers may cry foul. Imagine Inspector Maigret on a sunny street, no rain in the forecast, or Smiley's wife faithful, or Graham Greene's heroes unable to drink. Yet most of us argue that growth entails change, if not necessarily the reverse. And we grow wary of repetition, weary of the same speech patterns, characters, action, syntax. There's nothing new under the sun. (Except, the echo answers, the computer, the Jiffy Fix-it-Glu, robotics, the television series ABC premiered last week. And there's some truth in such an objection. The problem for the writer, then, is to find some sufficiently available innovative context for the old old truths.) But if you get it right, why not repeat—why force the phrase into new form? Anachrony: a passage *déjà lu*. That memory of learning to read, for example, comes from *Group Portrait: Conrad, Crane, Ford, James, and Wells*, a study of colleagueship and influence I published as far back as 1982. And bits and snippets of the rest derive from other pages—I plagiarize myself.

> The love of posthumous fame is a common psychological substitute for the love of perfection, even as the love of perfection may prove a projection into the world of art of a sense of guilt. The Astrologers find this love of perfection in those born under the sign of Virgo; it is to the artist as virginity to the nun and this love of purification they declare confined to those born between the end of August and the end of September. A writer should not be too conscious of such abstractions as perfection and posterity, 'the cackle of the unborn about the grave,' he should be above a flirtation with time, determined only to restore to the world in a form worthy of his powers something of what he has taken out.

Thus Cyril Connolly, in *Enemies of Promise*.

Each novelist, I think, must at some time be seized by a perception of the foolishness, not to say futility, of the enterprise: a grown person making up stories to gain other grown-ups' attention. We scuttle, pen in hand, to baseball games or bars and come back with our fragments of over-heard speech. We rise from our loved one's bed or hospital bedside and make notes; we enter delivery rooms or funeral parlors with the at least partly conscious intention of return-ing with a phrase. It's a strange profession and affords strange comfort: word-spinning, ghost-spelling, the King sung to sleep. That commonplace injunction to the appren-tice author, "Write about what you know," begs the question utterly: we discover what we know while writing, and it is more than we knew.

One duty of the writing teacher is to point out antecedents. "Tom, you might want to look at what Dick did with this plot device; Harriet, you might (re)read the novel by X, which your Y appears to follow." And more often than not the student has no notion that it's been tried before. Often the apprentice has not seen the model he or she so slavishly sets about to imitate. It's a kind of "Pierre Menard" in reverse and innovation as botanical procedure; "that which takes place at the apex of the thallus or leaf-bearing stem of mosses" is not conscious of or conscience-stricken by "the older parts dying off behind."

There's a way in which such ignorance is bliss—a precon-dition nearly of the imagination engaged. Ezra Pound's injunction "Make It New" predicates some knowledge of what was yesterday's news. Yet each of us when writing dreams of inventing the wheel.

When I was ten or eleven years old, I read and greatly admired *The Scarlet Pimpernel*. Baroness Orczy had it just right: the world was dressed in scarlet, and I was a disguised indolent-appearing hero. There were archenemies around every corner, determined to unmask me, and damsels in distress. Later, when I saw the movie, I wanted to be Leslie Howard. I jumped out of closets and up behind couches in my parents' house, singing the Pimpernel's song:

They seek him here, they seek him there,
Those Frenchies seek him everywhere.
Be he in heaven, be he in hell,
That damned elusive Pimpernel.

Then I'd twirl imaginary moustachios, put thumbs in my silk waistcoat, and sidle out of the room. I loved the book and praised it to anyone who'd listen, to several who agreed. At sixteen or so I praised it to a teacher who said the book was awful, and I shouldn't waste my time with pretentious prose. I told him he was wrong; he told me to read it again. I did, or tried to; he was correct. *The Scarlet Pimpernel* is of a piece with today's bestselling bodice-rippers; it candy-coats reality, its prose is purple and its every sunset roseate; I could not read the book now.

There are certain authors, of course, who appeal to both the young and old, who may be read with profit at whatever age. But Baroness Orczy is not of that company, nor did she try to be. My present disdain of her work does not erase the fact that once I cherished it. Those parents who consider their childhood's music magical and the music of their own children dull forget this: we relinquish models as we grow.

It helps to have models, however—to pattern a book along previously drawn lines. So Joyce with *Ulysses*, and Homer before him, arranging formulae. The whole notion of originality is modern and, to a degree, aberrant; it bothered Shakespeare not at all. The great majority of his work has sources elsewhere: the artist as magpie, with bits and threads of other texts to line his nest.

But what he makes of Holinshed, or Plutarch, or voyage accounts! The more one studies his originals, the more surprising he seems. Of the conspiracy, for instance, in *Henry IV, I*, Holinshed has only this to say: "Edmund Mortimer Earl of March, prisoner with Owen Glendower, whether for irksomeness of cruel captivity or fear of death or for what other cause it is uncertain, agreed to take part with Owen against the King of England, and took to wife the daughter of the said Owen."

What a world of things unsaid, of blanks to be filled in: "The lady sings in Welsh."

One definition of maturity may be the absence of influence—or the balanced deployment thereof. This is not to deny enthusiasm: *en theos*, the penetrating God. But the burden of the past becomes less consequential as the prospect of sequence, *con*sequence grows routine. It's not, I think, an accident that autobiography's an aging author's game—or that of the young writer, stuck like a fly to the strip of the self. We become our own antecedents, our *aboriginals*: child fathering the man. "Tradition and the Individual Talent" in this context comes to mean a mirror held to nature's mirror, taking pride of place.

Those Janus-faced futurists: Proust, Joyce, and Mann. How many years ago the "modernist canon" was produced: *Buddenbrooks, Lord Jim, The Ambassadors, The Waste Land, Ulysses, Sons and Lovers, To the Lighthouse, The Cantos, The Sun Also Rises, The Sound and the Fury*—such a list reveals its maker. All are much more than fifty years old, and many now near a hundred; in actuarial terms, they should long be dead. Like "ravel," a word that entails its own undoing, "generation" is a one-word oxymoron: that which starts and ends.

I published my first novel when twenty-three; five years thereafter, I wrote a screenplay for the book. We were in production in Rome. I had not carried the novel along, had said "Goodbye to All That"—or so I announced to the starlet and director when they asked. The truth was I could not remember, would lock myself into the room at the Pensione and try to reconstruct not only dialogue but even the characters' names.

It did not work. One day I entered a bookstore near the Spanish Steps—a secondhand bookstore with a large English-language section. There, in the familiar pale blue jacket, was my novel. I bought it. It turned out to be a presentation copy—though I could not remember the dedicatee, a "Dan" to whom I'd signed it over. Providential, this return: the reinvented screenplay went much more smoothly now. I could consult the past. There were certain passages it made sense to retain, certain phrases and exchanges that could, verbatim, persist. We finished the screenplay, and I returned to America while they went to Sicily to shoot.

The end of the story is quick. They made the movie but not in my version, retaining just the novel's name. I need not have reread it at all.

My parents spoke German together; my mother was proud of her accentless French. They could quote Goethe, Schiller, Heine—whereas the books that I read as an American schoolboy meant little or nothing to them. We were not religious, had no texts by heart. So I can only imagine what it would feel like to have a natal literature—to know the Book of Common Prayer, Piers Plowman, Chaucer, Fielding, Austen, Byron, and the rest as birthright, as something my ancestors read. I do not know the Talmud either, and read German and French through a glass darkly.

This is not meant to cry foul, or to act the cultural orphan; the circumstance is so widespread as to be the rule. Yet those black writers who grow expert in African literature, those feminists who uncover forgotten books by women can seem forlorn at times in their hunt for ratification. As if some voice might call to them from the yellowing pages: you too, *mon semblable, ma soeur.*

The pleasures of rereading derive in part from a sense of tradition received—that somewhere in some previous context the same book was read by a stranger. Since we happen to have been that stranger (in our four- or forty-years-previous guise), remembrance grows all the more poignant: here's the name of an old lover on the inside flap, the marginalia we cannot remember having written but recognize as ours, the appointment or telephone number it once seemed so urgent to keep.

Now there's merely memory, and often inexact. *Could* Queequeg swim; *did* Andrew and Natasha live happily together; *when* does Rosemary sleep with Dick Diver, and in which hotel? It's not so much a question of the purity of the original enterprise as of its sanctity. However second-rate the first performance we watch of a play, it remains nonetheless our touchstone; however amateurish the illustrations in our first copy of Stevenson or Cooper, that's how we imagine the characters should look.

My wife and I were in Colombia when Gabriel García Márquez returned for the first time in years. We stayed in Santa Marta, the author's native town. *One Hundred Years of Solitude* had been recently acclaimed; he had been in exile but was, of a sudden, a national treasure, the world-famous author come home. What "Gabo" did was news. His sister's breakfast menu made the front section, inside-page first column of the newspapers in Bogota; his narrow escape from a taxicab's fender would rate front section, first page. No one could remember how many months "Macondo"—the song composed in his fictive township's honor—had been number one on the hit parade; the most expensive condominiums in the most expensive seaside resorts were called "Macondo" too. An Olympic bicyclist was, perhaps, more celebrated that week—but only perhaps, and then only barely; Márquez was the hero as bard.

It was as though a people came to consciousness because written—a place became of consequence because described. The epic impulse, in short: we exist, and have our singer. This has something to do, surely, with the relative homogeneity of Colombia and its smaller size than this its northern neighbor. But imagine how far we have come from the plausible bard; no North American author today could dream of such success. We are invited to government functions, if at all, as window dressing; we appear in the media briefly if at all. The bestselling "serious" author makes as much per annum as a rock star in a week. We take inconsequence for granted, flattering ourselves—in bars, beds, symposia—that time will turn us consequential nonetheless.

When I read the announcement of Hemingway's death I was eighteen years old and alone for the first time in Paris. It was the start of July. The writer had died of a gunshot wound in Ketchum, Idaho, and *The International Herald Tribune* reported the story circumspectly: we did not know the details yet, knew only the result. *Our most important author, our laureate, our lion*—in 1961 his reputation had not dimmed; the praise was universal and the work revered.

Like many others of my generation, I had read him avidly; "Papa" was the father of us all. His early stories and novels, his definition of style as "grace under pressure"; his notion that a man of words could also be a man of action—all these were true and fine. Nick Adams, Frederick Henry, Robert Jordan—not to mention Lady Brett and the beautiful Catherine Barclay—set imagination's standard: *this* is the way you must hunt, drink, and court, *this* is the way to behave. Since I hoped to be a writer, they also looked like signposts: *this* is the pathway and *this* is the gate, *this* the spoor to track. Later I would follow a host of other authorial leads, but Hemingway began it; he was the heavyweight hero, he had caught the biggest fish and married the most wives and been the writing champ. . . .

We knew what he looked like in photographs and sounded like in interviews; we knew his personal history (the "dangerous summer" of bullfights, the various war wounds and airplane crashes and accidents) and that he sharpened pencils at the writing desk and, because of a bad back, worked standing up. When you lie for a living long and well enough, the line of demarcation between fancy and fact does tend to blur. He became his own invention in the news and on the page. I never did meet him, of course, but knew his nicknames—"Ernie," "Tatie," "Hem"—and familiar to the point of intimacy was his obsession with death.

So it seemed merely proper, in the city of *The Sun Also Rises*, to drink to the author's memory. "Let's have some irony and pity here," I told myself. "Let's get tight." I had been staying in a cheap hotel on the Rue des Écoles, walking distance from those Left Bank cafés he celebrated: Le Select, the Café Flor, the Dôme. I drank a *coup* of *vin ordinaire*, drank two. Then out again along the Boulevard Raspail and into the Luxembourg Gardens where I was, it turned out, not alone. Young men were mourning their lost leader and bending elbows everywhere and donning sunglasses tragically, saying "Yes, isn't it pretty to think so" to anyone who listened at the several bars. As though running the bulls at Pamplona, we weaved back down the Boulevard St. Germain to the ancient church he'd written of and sat in its cool shade.

This memory begins with the first person pronoun, and it *did* feel personal. His death was public property, and it could be shared. Soon enough there would come the postmortems, of both artist and career. We would learn the wound was self-inflicted, learn of his inability to write after electroshock treatment and his paranoia and sad final years.

And so the tune would change. What once had seemed heroic came to look like pomp and bluster; what had been an example to imitate became one to avoid. The macho posturing or, as Max Eastman put it, cult of "false literary hair on the chest" looked more and more like "Bull in the Afternoon." Hemingway had peaked too early, he had lost his influence as well as mind and nerve. He had been important once, had flourished and faded and was an object lesson in failure, not success.

Truth resides between. There's a famous anecdote about the early work and how it came to be lost. Though penniless and at penury's edge, Hemingway and his first wife always seemed somehow to fetch up on the Riviera or in Spain, and during one such winter—1922—he went ahead to Switzerland. Hadley joined him there. He had asked her, it would seem, to bring along his work in progress from the flat in Paris, and she packed it dutifully, taking all the drafts and carbons in a separate valise. "During the very brief time when the bags were out of her sight," as his biographer Carlos Baker reports, "the valise with the manuscripts was stolen."

Hadley was inconsolable; he too. The loss became an emblem for what proved irretrievable: his hopeful youth, his marriage, his sense of possibility, his early close wrangling with words. Years and decades later he could not bear to speak of it, as though Eden were ransacked that day and he himself expelled. And everyone who helped him—Gertrude Stein, Ford Madox Ford, F. Scott Fitzgerald and the rest—are dismissed in *A Moveable Feast* with retrospective savagery; it's as though the fierce old man rewrote the journeying boy. There's a noticeable divide in that final book of his between the sun-shot and nostalgia-splashed description of the early career and its bitter aftertaste.

Still, I have my suspicions. We cannot know, in truth, if what she misplaced on the train was the apprentice's work or the precocious master craftsman's—if imperishable language or mere penny-ante prose was lost. Perhaps he found the stories later and saw that they weren't any good. Hemingway's memory would have been accurate at twenty-three, his hand steady and eye clear; he could have reconstructed what was worth saving and scrapped what were anyhow scraps.

My best guess is that the suitcase did disappear but that he found a notebook and a draft or six nevertheless. In such a scenario some passages would have been recovered and thereafter recycled; it's possible that what he later called "the Paris stuff," with its romantic evocation of first love and first-discovered prowess, derived in part from those sketches; we tend to repeat our good lines. If history can be remembered, and if it belongs to the victors, why could he not revise the suitcase stories and call them a memoir?

What we cherish, secretive, are sampler sentiments. Auden puts it this way:

It is a sobering experience for any poet to read the last page of the Book Section of the Sunday *Times*, where correspondents seek to identify poems which have meant much to them. He is forced to realize that it is not his work, not even the work of Dante or Shakespeare, that most people treasure as magic talismans in times of trouble, but grotesquely bad verses written by maiden ladies in local newspapers; that millions in their bereavements, heartbreaks, agonies, depressions, have been comforted and perhaps saved from despair by appalling trash while poetry stood helplessly and incompetently by.

The academy has something to do with all this also. Haven and employer for the novelist, it provides a friendly soil for academic texts. The teacher finds it easier to speak of "complicated" books than simple ones, to treat them as ciphers to crack. "Let's see where the Kabbalah enters in; let's discuss the recurrence of the teacup motif; let's find the Jungian archetype in this subordinate clause." Add the pleasure of puzzle-solving to the *frisson* of the confessional and you have complicated books about the bookish life. Characters deal with each other as characters; dialogue contrives to be both eloquent and arch; the artifact itself becomes of consequence. Read *me me me me me*.

The childhood game of telephone: a message passed from lip to ear, whispered in a circle till the final player must announce what he's been told. And how we laugh at difference, the word golf, the misunderstanding and garbled transmission and change. . . . How suggestive what we hear, how telling what we miss! That last receptor, smiling, shamefaced, trying to pretend it wasn't his fault really, blaming the girl to his right, the lisp and breathy gargle three mouths down—that final player is the novelist: time's fool, tradition's mime.

The Lost Suitcase

A NOVELLA

He had been urging Hadley to fly down whenever she felt "travelly." The prospect of dodging among the snowy mountains was not very tempting and she took the train instead. But the journey was made under conditions so harrowing for her and so horrible for Ernest that neither of them was ever able to forget it. . . . During the very brief time when the bags were out of her sight, the valise with the manuscripts was stolen.

—Carlos Baker, *Ernest Hemingway: A Life Story*

ONE

I picture it this way:

She gets off the train.

She looks expectant and lovely and perhaps a little flustered, since she has not seen her husband in five weeks. She carries a handbag and duffel and worn leather suitcase and hatbox and small steamer trunk and also a string sack filled with pâté and oranges and cheese. Her light brown hair lifts in the breeze. What she wears is unimportant, since this is a woman whose clothes suggest removal: a brown woolen skirt with a side slit, a closely woven Irish V-neck sweater of an indeterminate color best described, perhaps, as mauve. She sports her trademark bombardier jacket also, the one her husband gave her in the period of courtship, and that he claimed he'd "liberated" at the end of the Great War. Although she has been up all night, her skin has the fine flush of youth.

We are not, it should be noted, in one of those glass-roofed overarching metropolitan stations where a multitude of trains arrive and the voyager negotiates a bustling glut of strangers. No busy hum of commerce here; no colloquy of engines. Rather, these are village scenes: a station with a single track for eastbound and a single track for westbound trains, and a footbridge with a semaphore and bank of signal lights exposed to every weather. We have arrived in countryside; the birds that swoop and hover are not city birds, not pigeons. They make their nests on pine boughs, not steel girders under glass.

Smoke dissipates; so does the shriek of the steam whistle and the harsh exhalation of air from the brakes. This train is composed of five cars. Between the dining and the baggage car there are only three for passengers—one first class carriage, two second. Doors slam; the conductor leaps down. Now he turns and, with a practiced gesture, offers disembarking travelers—parents with their children, and the infirm and the elderly—his hand. An old man with a walking stick half-stumbles, stepping out; then he straightens and with a gloved finger adjusts his black Homburg and, resolutely upright, limps away.

Pausa.

She gets off the train.

We should infer from the brief interval not that our lady descends from the car in exhaustion or indifference but that the number of bags she carries impedes her easy exit and she has waited politely for the unencumbered to leave. She hands the conductor her hatbox and steamer trunk and duffel and, by the time he turns once more, having deposited these items, has stepped to the platform unaided. As if in compensation for the fact she did not take his hand, she rewards him with a smile. He tips his cap and turns away; he would linger with her gladly but has his work to do. For it is his present duty to assist those customers who would ascend the stairs from which she has lately descended, and to make certain they do so in order.

Glad cries of recognition in the background, reader; shouts of welcome; waved farewells.

She takes a small step forward. Her ankles are sturdy yet thin. Now, in that instant with which all who journey are familiar—and, it would appear, particularly those whose habitual form of locomotion is the locomotive—she hesitates, uncertain, unable to determine if the movement underneath her feet is that of her own forward progress or of the platform itself. It belongs, perhaps, to each. When Albert Einstein (not so very far from here or long before) determined that all things are relative and that the motion of the spheres, which once great Ptolemy described as music, may be more properly defined as perception (you move while I remain immobile; we advance together; I start and you stop)—when Einstein raised his downcast gaze from the paper-strewn library table in Berne he might well have noticed just such a person on the street beyond his window, fixed yet mutable. He was myopic, after all, and often by his calculations abstracted, but never so completely as to miss a pretty face. Her breasts too would have merited attention; her name is AnnaLise.

Activity. Distraction. The stationmaster checks his watch—a gold half-hunter on a chain—and, with a wave of his right hand, signals his approval to the thick-moustachioed and smiling engineer. That worthy returns the salute. A-OK. In this Alpine village each arrival is of consequence, even in its own small way and, although it happens twelve times daily, an event. The train is precisely on time.

And what of the platform itself? There are wooden benches and a tin-roofed overhang, for no doubt in winter the snowfall lies deep. A pile of sand and cinders, heaped against the prospect of the next storm's ice-slick footing, has been mounded by a snow fence; a shovel reposes there jauntily also, jammed in the pile to the hilt. It protrudes at, say, forty degrees. Its visible handle is brown. The traces of snowmelt continue to glisten by the north-facing wall of the engineer's shed—green-shingled and red-roofed, with fretted carving on the eaves and an ornamental weathervane. The stovepipe requires fresh blacking; it has been permitted to rust.

A lone porter smokes in the sun. Spring sun. His yellow-billed cap is pulled low on his brow. His boots are dust-dimmed black. A flower vendor stands ready to meet the noon train, as does a man selling newspapers (the *Zurischer Zeitung*, the *Allgemeiner Tagesblad*), and there is a kiosk for pretzels and pickles and beer. Its shutters, however, are closed. The cafeteria inside the station proper has been open since eleven-thirty, offering lunch, and a single proprietor—Anders M. Hoffman, his name emblazoned on the menu—operates both. At such an hour of the day, or so he confides to his cousin, it makes no decent business sense and would be the grossest stupidity to act as his own competition, because the markup in the cafeteria is greater and the food more various and we have not yet reached, *Gott sei dank*, that condition of modernity where customers prefer to stand while eating and men begrudge a tip. His specialty is cheese fondue, with caraway seeds and kirsch and dark thick-crusted bread; he also

offers a *berühmte croque-monsieur.* He has four children, one
a cretin, and on Saturday night at the end of the work week
Anders M. Hoffman beats his wife.

A dog lies by a wooden wheelbarrow, dreaming, its tail
twitching. The train whistle sounds; the bell clangs. Schoolchildren on their way home for the midday meal file past.
Fitfully, noisily, steam is released, and now what AnnaLise
remarks upon is shrouded, veiled by steam.

Zermatt. Interlaken. Gründelwald. Wengen. Zaas-Fe. I
don't know the names of the stations, in truth, or at least
not their sequence and which would belong to what line. All
that matters at this point is image and feeling; later, I'll do
the research. What matters is color and shape. The brown of
her hair, for example, matches that of the parcel a priest lets
negligently dangle from his right hand in the lower far right
corner of the composition; the red of her coral necklace is
the red of the lettering on a placard we cannot quite deci-
pher to the left.

Once more, a whistle shrills. The wheels move perceptibly forward, then back. White mountains loom ahead. *I think
I can I think I can I think I can,* the little engine tootles. In
this complicated equipoise of arrival and departure AnnaLise
stands irresolute, searching; she'd assumed that her husband
would meet the noon train. They'd planned it, of course;
they'd agreed. In his most recent telegram he said he could-
n't wait. Is he hoping to surprise her; is he hiding; might he
be late? Is he leaning, as he often does, at the counter of
some zinc-topped bar, trading stories with the bartender and
finishing his schnapps? Is he so engrossed in the newspaper
or, better yet, in his own work of writing that he has forgotten the time? In the telegram itself he'd used their private
love talk; he'd written *Liebchen Come Stop It's Wonderful
Here Stop Come Right Now Don't Stop.*

Remembering, she raises her hand to her throat. AnnaLise
is not a prude and indeed is passionate by nature and particularly so about her husband; they have been married three
years. She delights in providing him pleasure, and has there-
in discovered her own. She has missed him beside her each

night. Yet his habits of speech disconcert her, and the way he does not seem to mind who listens when he urges her to piece by piece remove her clothes, and how he likes to name every individual part of her body as though for an appreciative audience, from toe to ear, from instep to chin, from rib to clavicle, and how he does not seem to care if strangers hear and turn to stare or if the thin partitions of their lodging house fail to muffle the shrill squeak of bedsprings and the enthusiastic roaring he indulges in in bed.

She peers about more urgently. Nobody. *Niemann. Personne.* Is she nearsighted, perhaps? Should she be wearing glasses and is it a small vanity that she hides them in her handbag, or does her fixed glazed gaze suggest—pardonable, surely, in one so young and far from home—some half-conscious and unexpressed fear? Later, we will decide. We will watch her studying a menu or a distant mountainside and thereby determine the range of her vision, but at this moment it's irrelevant: you and I also would stare. For blinking in the glacial sun and craning her long slender neck, turning, shifting, cold of a sudden within her warm jacket and securing with a practiced gesture its uppermost button and bombardier flap, AnnaLise repeats the action (though there is no one here to notice) that enflames her husband so, rotating her head back and forth as though the ambient air itself were her down-filled and lilac-scented and yielding yet supportive pillow. Her cheekbones are pronounced. Her lustrous brown eyelashes curl; her eyes are blue-flecked hazel and the pupils large.

Still another of her small enchantments is a lack of self-assurance, and for an instant she permits herself to wonder if perhaps she got the name of the station wrong, or the particular day. Her first impulse, tellingly, is to blame herself, not him. His name is Edward; he calls himself Ed; her name for him is *Schatz*.

It is time, now, to mention the clouds. Cirrus and cumulus both. We have earned a moment's respite and can cast about and see the sky, see high gray clouds the shape of geese massing northerly—the direction of the weather—in the top right quadrant of our canvas, although the outer edge remains bright blue. Whatever storm is coming—witness the shovel, the mounded sand—will take hours to appear. And since every motion must entail an equal and opposite motion (so writes Uncle Albert at his desk, remembering his predecessor Isaac Newton, musing on the dialectic of the future and the past and its vivid synthesis, this momentary present), our train departs apace. Once more the whistle, steam, and smoke, once more the clanging bells. All those who wish to have clambered aboard; all those who are leaving have left.

Where *is* he, where are you, my love? AnnaLise stares down the length of the platform, in both directions, east and west, then also at the footbridge and the empty platform opposite. She has been hunting his familiar form, his athlete's striding gait. Perceptibly the crowd around her thins—the priest, the schoolchildren, the stationmaster and businessmen—until she remains with the porter and dog. The former lights another cigarette, for he has no customers; the latter lies asleep. It is mostly shepherd, its muzzle white with age. What dream it dreams we cannot know, but there are rabbits in it surely and perhaps, in the meadow, a fox.

Tentative bird call. Resumption of birds. If we listen we may hear the dog's sharp snuffling intake and loud exhalation of breath. The porter, stretching, yawns. In the comparative silence that ensues, AnnaLise collects herself (a strange expression in this context, but appropriate, for it is not *controls* herself, not an act of self-control but rather a subliminal and metaphoric *gathering*) and overhears, within the building proper, the sounds of conversation and laughter and the tinkle and chink of glass and plate, and thinks perhaps he waits within, having secured a table, or perhaps has left a message, and so she picks up her luggage and shoulders her way through the door.

Red door. Red wooden door. Red wooden swinging door with two glass panes.

Our attention, reader, has been perforce on her, not him, and therefore this next entrance can be brief. Ah, this comedy of errors and series of mistakes! Of course Ed has remembered—how could he not, why would he not?—and set off for the village with sufficient time to spare. Of course he plans to meet the train and take her in his arms again and lead her home and then upstairs and resume, as it were, *la vie passionée*. But there were oxcarts on the road and trees felled by the weight of snow and the car he borrowed from the local baker for the occasion burst a tire two kilometers from anywhere, and by the time he'd fixed it he was late.

Not very late; not unforgivably so. He parks by the side of the track. He arrives at the platform, let us agree, three minutes after AnnaLise has stepped inside the building in the hope of finding him. Her eyes have grown accustomed to the smoke-filled comparative dark, while she ascertains to her dissatisfaction that her husband is not in the room, not standing at the bar or talking to the ticket seller or purchasing a magazine or a gift box of chocolates or sitting at a table in the half-empty cafeteria. Wavering, she asks herself if she should order coffee and pass the time until the next train comes to town—when? how long would she be forced to wait?—or attempt instead to seek the help of some friendly local and with her meager travel funds arrange her own conveyance to the place he has been writing in and from which he has written so often and enthusiastically, saying it is not expensive, saying it is quiet here, saying the skiing is fine. While all this transpires, I imagine, he questions the porter (The train, has it come?) and, when the porter nods (*Gewiss, mein Herr*), with what we will learn to recognize as his own characteristic and antithetical (to his wife's, I mean, though others would in later years remark upon it equally) self-assurance, Edward strides the length of the platform, then turns on his heel and pushes through the very door she so tentatively opened not five minutes since.

Electric lights. A wooden floor. Two ticket windows with bars. Benches ranged around the walls and schedules posted under glass and an unlit coal stove in the corner where in the winter we huddle for warmth. The hum and buzz of lunchtime has resumed. Those men inside the station who observed AnnaLise enter, briefly, surreptitiously, have returned to their food and their talk, for this is Switzerland after all, not Italy or France, and the presence of an unaccompanied and attractive woman in their midst is not something to remark upon out loud. And whatever their private reckoning—whatever hopes of dalliance or proffered service or adventure they might entertain—they are not of course surprised when a man arrives to claim her, when he speaks her name and she, turning, with a half-suppressed exclamation of pleasure and a smile of sweet relief, throws herself into his arms.

They kiss. They kiss again. Would it be seemly now to focus on the physical exchange of intimate endearments?—how she presses up against him and he feels the first stirring of blood in his groin, how his strong arms compress her breasts and how she whispers yieldingly that she's so happy happy happy to be here at last, he's looking wonderful, so brown, so much like a pirate with his new Van Dyke, it grows so thick, it is such a surprise, and how he then explains the unexpected business of tire changing and the difficulties of the road but he's sorry sorry sorry and he should have known enough in this *verdammte* country to expect the unexpected, she too is looking wonderful, he can't believe his luck. He is a tall man; she nuzzles his neck. Does it prickle? he asks her; do you really like it? should I shave? Oh yes, she says, oh no. Let's get you out of here, he says, let's get you where we'll be alone, oh *Schatz*, she breathes, yes, let's.

He picks up the duffel and the string sack and the hatbox and the steamer trunk. The suitcase? Edward asks. She has promised to bring it, of course. She has done just what he wants. He has requested chèvre also, the particular leaf-wrapped double *graisse* that they particularly liked from the *épicerie* across the street, and also of course his American mail, but what he most desires and requires are his handwritten manuscripts and notebooks and typescripts, and she has carried them along with her as though they were pure gold. The suitcase contains all his stories; it is the sum and substance of his career so far, the claim he stakes on artistry and the mark he plans to make. When her husband went ahead to find lodgings in the Engadine, to establish a place where he might work and they could afford to live cheaply and well, at least all spring and summertime until the money gave out or what he produced was sold—when he went ahead to ski and write and scout out their location AnnaLise remained behind and gave a month's not so much *notice* as *opportunity* to Madame LaBecque, their landlady and a milliner for whom she sometimes modeled hats and whom she sometimes helped behind the counter, since her gratitude was genuine and their family friendship long-standing. Madame LaBecque, said the doctor, could be cured by bed rest but she must not stand all day or she would suffer a relapse as surely as I'm standing here, so AnnaLise had told her husband, I'll close up the flat, darling, I'll finish up—and though she missed him terribly the missing was annealed by pleasure at the thought that he was working, was productive and missing her also, equally.

Then when he wrote at last to say he'd found them a chalet among fir trees with a wide horsehair mattress and an embroidered duvet and a window with a view and a desk, and she should come and bring along his stories, please, and whatever else she thought they'd need but all he needed, now, was her, she, AnnaLise, was overjoyed and booked the train from Paris and acquired the chèvre he asked for, and in her duffel in between the skirts and V-neck sweaters and pair of ankle-high walking shoes she folded the red stockings he especially fancied. And then she collected his stories, his wonderful stories, his genius stories, from the drawer he had piled them in and, following instructions, packed every single draft of them and all the carbons also into his leather suitcase and secured them with a double strap as well as the padlock and key.

These items she took on the train.

These she removed from it, surely.

She could not sleep from dusk till dawn, too excited and watchful to rest. But, standing in the station lobby, before they think to go outside and check again, before they pace the platform and consult the porter, before they look within the wheelbarrow where, with a small surge of expectation, they discover an unwrapped and abandoned parcel but not, alas, his (a much-thumbed newspaper, a broken pencil, a mostly eaten sandwich left behind, it may surprise us to discover, by the priest), and long before they have determined that misplacement is displacement and, as it does not take an Einstein to inform us, loss irrecoverable, while still holding to her husband's hand AnnaLise takes a rapid shocked inventory of the luggage that remains—the string sack filled with oranges, the handbag, the duffel and the hatbox and the blue steamer trunk—and registers with what is disbelief at first, and then a growing certainty, then horror, that the suitcase, the suitcase, the *suitcase* is gone.

Why should she carry the pâté and cheese; what use is her garter belt now? What possible pleasure will oranges yield, now that his stories are lost?

We could go on in this fashion but won't. The reader has noticed, perhaps, how much has been elided here, how many questions have been begged. For instance, nationality; what kind of name is AnnaLise? Or, for that matter, Edward, Ed; why does she call him Schatz? *For instance, the precise location in the Engadine and whether the train was a sleeper and who was traveling first class. Is she pregnant; if so, does she know? If she carries a child, is it his?*

This morning I hear their discussion:

Oh, *Schatz*, it's my fault.

No.

I'm such a fool.

I should have been at the station to meet you.

I'm such a fool, she repeated. Oh, everything, it's all *my* fault.

It'll turn up.

Do you think so?

Of course. It's just a suitcase.

Yes.

And this is Switzerland. Nobody steals a suitcase here. Not one like mine. They'll give it back.

She touched his arm. It has your stories in it.

Yes.

They'll read them and they'll think they're wonderful and they'll call up the stationmaster and say, Who was that genius?

No they won't.

Who was that genius who wrote those stories and how can I contact him, please? They deserve to be in print.

Or maybe he's a publisher.

Who?

The man who took my suitcase. The one who's been reading my work.

Yes, that's right, he's from Gallimard. Or possibly Hachette. He's the editor in chief.

And he'll call us in the morning and he'll say *Chapeau.*

Of course he will.

They all will. The entire board of directors. They'll send a telegram: *Chapeau.*

Darling, I could kill myself.

Don't say that. Just think about how good we'll feel tomorrow when the suitcase is returned.

Oh *Schatz*, I don't deserve you.

No.

I'll try to, I promise. Tonight.

Yes.

Or this afternoon. Right now. This very instant. As soon as we get out of here.

We'll file a claim.

Yes. Yes, that's right.

We'll inform the stationmaster. He'll telegraph ahead.

Let's tell him now.

We'll post a reward.

By all means, let's post a reward.

We'll tell him these were official papers. And the suitcase contains major secrets of state. And he has to stop the train and conduct a search and return it immediately, on pain of death.

Death?

Well, treason anyhow.

Don't joke about it, darling. I feel rotten enough as it is.

It's not your fault.

Yes. Yes it is.

Don't let's think about it and don't let's talk about it.

I've done this to you, haven't I?

Let's have a drink, he said.

If you want to.

I need a drink, Edward said.

Absolutely.

Or two or three.

Yes. Let's get stinko together.

By all means. What will you drink?

Is the station's lit interior too substantial for the sleepy small hamlet described, or would that be appropriate in Switzerland in 19—?

Would there be electric lights? How long since "The Great War"?

Was the suitcase collected on purpose or through inattention; did it get lifted to the train again or hauled by some local away?

Are its contents as established above, and do they have intrinsic value or is it simply the sentimental impulse of an apprentice artist that he should keep the clumsy tentatives, his first thick-thumbed efforts at prose?

What other versions might obtain; what else is going on?

I picture it this way:

AnnaLise gets off the train.

She has been traveling all night and is not in the best of humors, not in good humor at all. There was no room in the first class carriage, not even in the WagonLit, and the man across from her kept rubbing up against her leg and smoking those bloody Gitanes. He had been eating bratwurst also, or knockwurst or one of those bloody German sausages in waxed paper with cabbage and mustard and *kartoffelsalat*, and wiping his hand on his shirt. She had had no plans to travel, or at least not in this manner and direction, but her husband sent a telegram. He had telephoned and written and then he sent his telegram at the worst possible moment, as always, so importunate and needy that she told the Count she'd better go; she'd have to tell Ed face to face that what he was was finished and their marriage a mistake. The Count himself was unperturbed; he poured them each a second cupful of Château d'Yquem. The cups were silver, embossed with his crest—a lion rampant, with a laurel wreath around its ears, and the image of his castle lightly etched beneath the lip.

She had never much cared for Yquem. It was sweet yet sour-tasting, thin, and the silver cups were wrong for it, and instead what she wanted was brandy or maybe a glass of champagne. What she liked best about the Count was his inner essential aloofness, the way he was a bastard and didn't care who noticed, the way he made her shine his boots and then brought her off with his brush. So when she said, I have to go, it's the one thing I promised him, he wants his bloody manuscripts, her lover did not seem to mind and raised those astonishing eyebrows of his and shrugged and offered wine. What *he* was was indifferent, and this excited AnnaLise, and so she made him lie back down and sucked him till he stiffened nicely and then she made him fuck her standing up. His prick was short and stubby, with a yellow tinge to it, and the hair around his balls was growing gray. She had asked him, once, what made that scar, the ragged one along his hip, the high-welted one that ran up to his ribcage—and he said he couldn't remember, it was a hunting accident, or maybe that time with a bull. Bull*shit*, she told him laughingly, how is it possible you can't remember, and he said—serious, for once—There are certain matters it behooves one to forget.

Behooves, that was his word. The unexpected formality, the way he did not smile while saying it, reminded her that the Count's English was a foreigner's or maybe even Jewish but anyhow not native and had been acquired in school. He was very rich, or so it seemed, and always there were chauffeurs waiting or servants to bring up the wine. Always there were hampers with lobsters and, all that winter, oysters and complicated sex toys and powder he said derived from his own private rhinoceros horn, the charging white rhino he'd bagged on the trip to Nairobi.

When she asked him what he meant by *bagged*, he said, Shot, my dear, brought down.

But his accent was peculiar, and she never knew exactly where it came from or exactly what he would get wrong. Yquem, Esau, Yconquered, was the toast that he liked to propose. And afterward, he liked to say, My dear, you look ravished tonight.

With her husband she felt far too old; with the Count she still felt young. Certain men are born with knowledge, and the Count, she knew, was born that way, but other men will die with everything to learn. Some men are born with aptitude, and the desire to learn quickly, and others have no aptitude no matter how hard they try. She had tried very hard to teach Edward, but now it was time to acknowledge she had absolutely failed. She was eight years his senior, and what went wrong between them had been no one person's fault and the thing they had together she understood now absolutely as a boy-and-woman affair.

They had met in the hospital three years before. He had had a bout of influenza and was feverish and spouting poetry and convinced she was an angel and that he would die. He babbled on about his family; his father was a doctor and used to take him fishing after something he called Walleye and then Tommy Trout and Micky Muskellunge and Billy Bass.

He was sure he'd never see his house in the suburbs or their camp in upper Michigan again; he ran on and on about green fields and Paradise and how she was an angel to be sitting there holding his hand. I'm a hell of an angel, she wanted to tell him, I'm here because I miscarried the baby some Tom or Harry's dick deposited before it went back home. Going back to your precious America, your dear old U.S. of A.

But when she was discharged she came back twice to visit him, and the second time she said all right, when you get well enough we'll go out for dinner, for dancing, whatever you want. Whatever he wanted, it turned out, was to walk along the Seine and lean on the bridges in moonlight and recite, with his atrocious accent, Baudelaire and Rimbaud and Verlaine. He believed in poetry and announced he wanted to write it, or prose. He believed that the best of the poets write prose, and also the reverse, because everything belongs together and is the attraction of opposites, and the two of them were perfect opposites, of course, and opposites attract. Their being together in Paris, he said, was an example of just this principle; it was romantic and astonishing and fine. Then he stepped back from the balustrade and said she looked angelic in the moonlight and the lamplight and would it be insulting if he asked her for a kiss?

She had felt sorry for him, she supposed, and even a little attracted to that great American uncertainty of his. She had felt sorry for herself as well, because the figure modeling and the film actress business were going nowhere fast. He had some money, it turned out, his doctor father sent him, and so they went to a hotel and though he was not technically a virgin he was virginal in all the ways that mattered, and by the time the morning came he asked her to marry him, please. Oh please oh please, he said, I'll do anything you want me to if you'll just answer yes.

Lise had not believed it, at first. She had been propositioned often enough but not often proposed to before, and not in a long time. Other people popped the question, and got down on their bended knees and waited for the object of their matrimonial desire to blushingly accede. The men she'd seen on bended knees had not been offering marriage exactly, and had not proffered rings. But this one refused to take no for an answer, and he asked her again the next morning, with a great bunch of roses in his fist and that great American-boy grin of his, and so she said, Oh what the hell, oh why not, let's give it a try.

They were married in a civil service in the Eighth Arrondissement, with a witness from the newspaper and a *notaire* who stroked her ass while she initialed documents, and then it was over and she was what they call an honest woman, Mrs. Ed. When she asked the blushing groom if they should send a telegram, if they ought to tell his family, he said, No, no, that would spoil it, I want to take you back to them as my wonderful surprise. What am I, a trophy, she wanted to ask him, a body you bring back alive? What am I, rhinoceros horn?

But by now he was reciting something English, by an Englishman, "Drink to me only with thine eyes," and then commenced to sing. All afternoon they had been drinking wine but after the ceremony they progressed to champagne; he told her the poem was also a song and tried to teach her the tune. I know some things, he said, about you, Lise. Your history. From now on, it's our song. She laughed and let him fondle her and they ordered the *notaire* and journalist another round. Then everyone drank to the newlyweds' health, and wished them every happiness and when he took his leave the *notaire* hoped that they might meet again, in private, since he had copied her address into his personal notebook. Then everyone emptied their glasses, *Salud y amor y pesetas; Salut, Sköl, Prosit*, and the *notaire* and the journalist left.

I understand some things, *Schatz* repeated, about you, wife. Your history. But of course he understood nothing whatsoever about her history and how it had not been about influenza or Jove's nectar or bejeweled loving cups, and certainly not a thirst that from the soul doth rise, and then he gave her the business about the eyes—large hazel blue-flecked pupils—being windows of the soul.

She had never had a brother, and she couldn't remember her father, and mostly who she went with had been older men. So for a while it was pleasant enough, and he had been enthusiastic about the things she needed to teach him, and he huffed and puffed and concentrated and did try to learn. To begin with she liked how he wanted to study, and how gratified he seemed to be by five minutes' worth of fucking and how speedily he came. He had some aptitude for knots, because of his time in the Michigan woods; he had some aptitude for knives, because of his time gutting fish. But Edward had no talent for the bed, he was absolutely without the gift for it, and their marriage spoiled as absolutely as what the Count called gut-shot game left lying in the sun. It had been rotten for months.

Of course he did not know this yet; he believed he was improving and did not appreciate or guess that he had been improved upon, or how very easy that had been to do. He was one of those great American boy-men, twenty-three years old tomorrow, and certain he would someday beat the world. He believed it was a race or fight and now that he was well again and had beaten influenza he was sure that he couldn't be beaten at all and would be a heavyweight champion, not only a contender. It was the way he talked. It was the sort of thing he said. He claimed she was his inspiration, his oh-I-say, his smashing girl, and that she should come along to Switzerland and Austria and be with him while he wrote. He was full of the desire to describe and then enlarge upon experience—unlike the Count, who would not speak about his exploits or his circumcision or how he acquired that scar.

Schatz talked a great deal about bravery, for example, and the need to act on impulse, which was what their marriage was and why they would be happy forever and ever together. But she had understood, of course, that he was engaged in bravado and only a boyish impulsiveness; he had seemed intent on writing but now all he did was revise.

So when he sent his telegram, saying, Come on down here, please, please come to me, I grew a beard, she had been planning to remain in Paris for the season or at least until

Biarritz. She had thought he understood that what was between them was finished, but he did not understand and needed to be told it to his face. She and the Count had commenced in September, at the races, after the races, yes, that evening in the trophy room and then in the tack room with saddles and stirrups, and there was no reason to break with the Count but she would break with *Schatz*.

So AnnaLise packed her husband's stories and his high school yearbook and his photograph of himself with a fish and what looked like an Indian standing behind him and also holding up a fish and squinting at the sun. She took her husband's shirts and socks and old appointment book and extra pair of pants and tie and scarf and balled them up and threw them together, his worldly goods, his youthful brave accomplishments, and stuffed them in the cracked leather suitcase so as to be rid of him entirely, entirely to shut him out, and then she locked the suitcase and pocketed the key. She hadn't really meant to go, except the Count said, Go ahead, and with his sleepy-lidded gaze was daring her to leave, of course, and so she had no choice but to accept the dare.

I'll deliver his schoolboy belongings and tell him, she said, I'll arrive there on his birthday and explain that the marriage is finished and that you're waiting here for me, and then I'll come right back.

The Count said, Yes, that's what we have for morality, that's what you ought to do. You'll be here, won't you, when I return, she could not keep from asking. Don't be ridiculous, he said, and then he told his chauffeur to drive Mademoiselle to the Gare.

So AnnaLise gets off the train. It's this bloody little village in the middle of nowhere, the *Engadine*, for chrissakes, and Edward's standing there all puppy-dog eager and ready to roll over and wag his tail and then sit up and beg. It's a platform with a cripple and a porter and a dog. There's dirty snow heaped by the tracks. In customs they called her, *Gnädige Frau*, and the man who collected her passport and looked at the photograph and then her face said, gallantly,

The photo doesn't do you justice, Madame, and tipped his blue cap and moved on.

That had been pleasant enough, but nothing else about the trip was pleasant, and she stood in the corridor staring at mountains and what they call, for some reason, chalets. The compartment had been hot and cramped and, even when she cracked the window, stale-smelling of onions and beer; the man with the bratwurst kept pulling down the curtain and planning, she could tell, to get demonstrative and she'd have to alert the conductor and it would be a scene. Or perhaps she would encourage her companion and say he was exciting her, such an impressive specimen, so manly, so attractive, and he should take off his pants. Then, while he did so, fumbling with his buttons, she would open the compartment door and invite other passengers in. But AnnaLise controlled herself (*collected*, possibly: is that the word?), and instead on the journey from Paris she thought about the Count, his way of laughing high up in his throat and how they had met at the races, hm, the races, yes, the races, that afternoon in Auteuil. She thought about his money and his accent and his manners, his beautiful manners, his stomach muscles like a washboard and the yellow tinge at the root of his cock and the way he did not give a damn whom he bought drinks for at the bar.

So she was feeling rotten, and thought about the night before, and it didn't help that Herr Von Bratwurst ogled her the whole way down from Paris and kept wiping his lips with his hand. Well, it had been her rotten luck to marry a man with everything to learn and no aptitude for instruction and to be sleeping now at last with one who knew it all. She stood a long time in the corridor, watching her reflection in the window in the tunnels and staring at the boy who sold coffee and chocolate and newspapers and sandwiches and drinks. He had the most amazing face, the face of an angel by Botticelli, and legs and arms she could not keep herself from imagining spread-eagled and then tied together with scarves. She had been an artist's model and she knew which pose to strike, what limb to bend in what direction and which was the come-hither look as opposed to the look that declared, *chien méchant*. With most men she controlled such things and understood how to make them behave; she knew what would shock or excite them, and which ones would be diffident or talented in bed. She could have managed Herr Von Bratwurst, for example, or the Botticelli sandwich boy, and she would manage her husband with no difficulty later. But the Count had challenged her, with his inner essential indifference, his assumption she too would forget their affair.

It's what we do, he'd said.

So that was what she tried to do, and she stood in the corridor staring at mountains and hearing the wheels on the track, clackety-clack, no going back, and rather despising herself. She was thirty-one years old and feeling a little bit sordid and things would have to change. A week from now or at the latest by the end of May the Count was planning to leave for Biarritz, and probably taking a woman along, or arranging for one with the driver, and it was over between them already and had never really begun. Her period was three weeks late and now what she had for morality was this errand to the wilderness, this decision not to seduce the chocolate-and-sandwiches boy and not to pretend to her husband that he had been her life's one love, or even close. She was glad Ed had found a vocation, and had found a thatched-roof cottage suitable for writing in, and suitable for Heidi, and she wished him well in it and hoped he would be a success. She believed in him absolutely, of course, and she would like to hear from him and hear about him in the future, but this was where she, AnnaLise, was getting off. And so she picked up her string sack and duffel and hatbox and small steamer trunk and, not waiting for the conductor, not saying anything to anyone, let herself down from the train.

Her great American boy-man awaits her. He is standing on the platform, in the sun.

You're here, he says. You're really here.

She acknowledges this, since it is true, and then he nuzzles and pecks at her neck, saying how glad he is that she arrived, how grateful that she made the trip and how long he's been waiting, how very much he missed her, and he borrowed a car to get down to the village although the way to travel, mostly, is on foot or skis or snowshoes and he's so very much looking forward to teaching her all about snowshoes and skis. The chalet they're staying in belongs to a family he assures her she will find enchanting, and of course they'll be enchanted by her also, and she's looking wonderful, wonderful, "Drink to me only with thine eyes," does she remember how they sang, and does she like his beard?

Schatz cannot believe his good luck. He's found the perfect place, he says, for only two dollars a day and with the fluctuation in the exchange rate his two dollars goes further each day, among great fir trees with a wood stove they use for heat and carvings on the outhouse that are just enchanting, wonderful, and wait until she meets the butcher and the baker in the village and listens to them sing. Oh wait until I get you there I can't wait, wife, can you?

There's nobody else at the station, or nobody worth mentioning—an old man limping up ahead, a porter rolling cigarettes, a fat self-important stationmaster peering at his watch. AnnaLise is feeling rotten, and more than a little bit sordid, and although she reminds herself that this is called morality and we might as well get it over with he babbles on and on the way he used to in the hospital and she can't interrupt.

Reader, we may do so; it is time to interrupt. I believe that the point has been made. Their names and faces are the same, but all else has been altered, and the station and its occupants, which loomed so large in the first scene, are unimportant now. Now what matters is experience, not innocence; what we witness is misunderstanding and, to a degree, remorse. In this draft we have a woman who holds all the marriage cards—a dominatrix, plausibly, since our Edward will be famous later for his love of pain—and who lays them flat on the table and says no deal, no dice. This AnnaLise is worldly and callous, not engagingly youthful or confused; this one has abandoned the suitcase as a point of principle or because she has forgotten it or simply does not care.

Did she not even bother to return to the compartment and collect the bag she knew must matter to her husband? Did I underestimate, perhaps, the trouble she has had with the man sitting opposite, his stale-sausage reek, and her consequent unwillingness to check the luggage rack? Does the question of the manuscripts obtrude at all upon her consciousness, or are the stories of no greater value to her than the yearbook and the photographs and socks? Might the customs agent have taken the object away for inspection, since a suitcase stuffed with documents is quite plausibly suspicious or at least an occasion for scrutiny and in violation of Rule 7, Paragraph 3?

So we require dialogue.

Descriptive prose.

The vanishing point of the platform; perspective; the source of the light.

And need to know: her height, his weight, the color of their hair. The fabric of the dress she chose when visiting the hospital.

That bombardier jacket, for example; would she wear it in this draft also?

The weather, the temperature and season. Is it in fact the first of May, and how may that be used? Are we in Austria, not Switzerland, and is this the noon train?

Would she be cold?

If Edward in this draft even ventured to request she bring the stories, or AnnaLise only threw them in as a prelude to throwing them out.

Why he, bedazzled, does not see at once that she does not have luggage.

How close our American author has come to dying not of a war wound but of disease. *(N.B. Locate the source of that contemporary jingle,* You opened the window, and influenza *and check the number of the dead from that pandemic: eighteen million? Twenty?)* and the way he will write about it later and whether or not the Count is Jewish and whether that should signify in the ensuing narrative and how many infidelities there may have been with the *notaire* and the journalist and others in the three-year interval before.

What day of the week it is. Monday?

Her family and if they were informed of the marriage and invited to attend or declined the invitation and if her mother and stepfather are alive.

And I must address the questions also of how long it takes *this* Edward to inquire of his consort what has happened to that leather container of language so important to him previously, and if Anders M. Hoffman should turn up again, perhaps together with the priest (the former a blasphemer, the latter credulous; the one a man who insists on his Sunday morning leisure abed after his Saturday evening debauch—if the Good Lord could rest on Sundays why can't his servant Anders? *Ach,* woman, stop that sniveling, just go to the *verdammte* church and take the children with you and tell him what a beast I am and let me have some peace and quiet if you please for once—the other a man who must ready himself in the cold solitary predawn dark to offer absolution to his cowed and beaten and in a statistically significant number of cases cretinous flock) and why her husband waits to ask if AnnaLise remembered to bring it, and their journey up the valley while she tells him she forgot.

But in any case and as before the suitcase has been lost.

TWO

Thirteen ways of looking at a suitcase:

1. As a container.
2. As the thing contained.
3. From above, across the handle (the handle itself of black leather, with frayed stitching and brass fit-

tings and small scratch marks made by the key while approaching the keyhole), the handle itself in your grasp.

4. Segmented by the luggage rack—across from or directly above our passenger?—divided by the soft striations of the yellow cord cross-hatching it and which, while supporting the object of our scrutiny, bellies from the metal struts, these struts at three-foot intervals or, because we are in Europe, a meter's distance each from each, so that what we witness now is weight suspended, nestled—nay, *nesting* there—as though this journey were a resting point and even perhaps a prelude to or form of flight, with the actual enterprise of travel soon to be resumed.

5. From the side.

6. From each of the five additional perspectives, since this rectangle or—because we have entered the world of solid geometry—parallelepiped consists of, in addition to its handle and buckles and strapping, six planes.

7. By the steamship labels pasted on, the chalk marks the customs men made. By the various stickers attached to it: the grand hotels and country inns, the Penzione and Albergi and SkiHofs and ports of origin or destination, the color-coded emblems of first or cabin or third class.

8. As a Christmas gift. Or birthday gift. Or graduation present. *Bon voyage.*

9. As a fashion statement. Whether worn, cracked, newly purchased, monogrammed, brown or black or tan or burgundy; by its obvious age or lack thereof; whether its corners have been reinforced or no; whether tasteful or vulgar, expensive or cheap.

10. In terms of size, not cost. The function as well as the form.

11. Because I've asked you to.
12. Because of what it means to him: his granddaddy's escape from Lübeck although not so much escape perhaps as willful pilgrimage, a decision taken in 18— and long since established as family lore; his father's way of telling him about granddaddy's farm, and how many things were different then, the way they used to be in this *verdammte* country once, before there were electric lights, before the telephone existed, not to mention the TV, and how they did their chores in every weather, rain or shine, in eighteen inches of snow sonnyboy, we walked five miles to school. In order to give *you* advantages, the things you take for granted, Ed, like running water and the telephone and this here suitcase used to hold, oh, everything your mother and I needed the year we started our own household, when I went off to medical school, and I'd like it if you were grateful, if you'd only show your gratitude and God bless America once.
13. As an occasion for and spur to speculation, a stimulus for just such a garden variety of cultural and historical and aesthetic and commercial inquiry, with a nod to Stevens's blackbird and also Faulkner's carpenter, Cash Bundren: my masters in the hall.

So I picture it this way:

She gets off the train.

And because my imagination has been, as is the case with all who belong to our lost generation, compelled and shaped by the movies, I see it on screen as a long shot and then as a close-up.

Lights, camera, action. Scene:

Smoke. Smoke clearing. The wheels of the engine. A piston. The platform. The station. Establishing shot. Enter the cameraman on the trolley, the director's daughter selling flowers, the producer's boyfriend playing the conductor, and then down-left the girl born in Topeka in the part of AnnaLise. Smoke again. The station clock. The stationmaster's watch. She is in fact a natural blonde, but her hair's in a pageboy and brown. Mauve sweater, skirt with a side slit, bombardier jacket, et. seq. (Questions: Does she belong to the leading or supporting actress category? Does she represent our first or second version of a traveler from chapter 1 or more probably some sort of an amalgam of the two? Is she seventeen or twenty-three or even thirty-one? Does it make any difference; what difference would it make? Because, as Gertie liked to say before a good fiesta, *Ihr gehören alle eine verlorene Generation an.*)

In this scene our actress cries. That's the point of it: *A. cries.* She should be holding back tears on the platform, then burst into tears when she sees him, then be inconsolable once in his arms. She must toss her head back in the light: eyes brimming, tears like Alpine snowmelt on a smooth expanse of cheek. When her husband inquires what's wrong she's too stricken to inform him; when he tells her that as long as they're together everything will work out fine she shakes her head piteously; when he says it can't be *that* bad, surely, she says oh yes oh yes it is; when he promises to fix it AnnaLise breaks down completely, sobbing No no no no no no.

It's not easy to look beautiful while weeping, or to do so on command for eight successive takes.

Between shots she must dry her eyes and make certain they're not swollen; she must compose herself and blow her nose and resume.

Take three.

Take four.

Take five.

For in any case our heroine has dreamed all through her adolescence, grade and junior high and high school, that there *must* be a world elsewhere and *something* else is possible and I've got to get out of here, *got* to, and then her big break came that time her drama teacher took the Drama Club to Chicago on a school trip in her junior year, because there was *Hamlet* and *Long Day's Journey Into Night* and *Oklahoma* all in one weekend and all in a package deal, and so everybody got to stay on the same floor in a hotel, and there was TV in the room and Billy found two cans of beer and they got giggly drinking it but when he tried to kiss her he had halitosis and afterward they went out walking and she kept touching her tongue to her braces and remembering his tongue there too, all that metal in her mouth her mother said she should be grateful for because her teeth will be, or so the orthodontist has assured them, perfect afterward, and her mother said you'll thank me, miss, whenever you look in the mirror you'll be purely grateful to your mother; meanwhile everywhere along the Loop there were all these amazing buildings and these amazing-looking people, so busy, so *directed*, and one of them did know their drama teacher and was part of Second City so she did get to sit in on what other acting companies might have described as a rehearsal but here was what they called a game, a theater game, and she could remember their names, their soon-to-be and in some cases already famous names, Paul Sills, Mike Nichols, Elaine May, Barbara Harris, and Paul Sands, because what we are after this morning, reader, is verisimilitude, a period piece, and therefore we require corroborative detail and buttressing data, and this would mean (assuming that the film was shot in the middle 1960s, say 196– or thereabouts, the years coincident with Edward's greatest commercial fame, although opinion has begun to shift and the critics grumble and express reservations and the serious readers already dismiss or devalue his work; still, in the period of which I write even his least important short story is the occasion for a bidding war, so "The Lost Suitcase" did get contracted for and adapted and cast and principal photography began in a torrential downpour in the railway station in Genoa in the third week of November, except there was the usual trouble during the production because the director had a heart attack, not fatal, and the story editor sought an injunction and the executive producer fired the cameraman and after the usual edits, *Sturm und Drang*, threats, counterthreats, hysterics, the film did get shot and mixed and ballyhooed and distributed and in *The New York Times* by Bosley Crowther panned) our girl was sixteen years old in the windy Second City when she had what she would later call a kind of conversion experience but is twenty-six today while she receives her first big break (so that the question of *which* AnnaLise she represents may be for the moment begged and the anterior question answered in the definite affirmative; she's our leading lady, it appears, not a supporting member of the cast, and what she must convey in this scene is despair, wordless misery, the haunted look of someone who has carried all night long the certainty of failure and the horror of the news she brings and the ensuing wreckage of her husband's confidence, his faith in her, their marriage, his career come crashingly to a caesura if not halt or stop, and in that regard must replicate the sprung interminable syntax of this very sentence, euphuistic, katechrestic, overwrit and overwrought, *take six, take seven, take eight, nine,* who has understood already and irrevocably that E. will not forgive nor she herself forget this loss, this inattention and betrayal in that moment she rehearses when the porter abandoned her suitcase); best not to look too closely at or to describe in overparticular detail the decade intervening, it's mostly a familiar story—work, play, vodka, trouble, dope, an aborted pregnancy, a seed-pearl necklace, a pet schnauzer, miniskirts—and so when she gets back home to Topeka from that first revelatory and, it is not perhaps too much to say, transformative weekend in Chicago she tells herself and her mother and everyone she *knew* she'd never ever quit until she became an actress, no matter what it takes. Took.

Or picture it *this* way:
    She gets off the train.

Her name is AnnaLise, his name is Edward, she has taken the sleeper from Paris; all this reads as before. The rest, as before, has been changed.

She is thirty-one, he twenty-three, and she cares about him in a fashion that's a compound of compassionate affinity and what for lack of other terminology we'll call maternal love. There is an element also of—how best to describe it?—physical ease if not desire; she likes lying beside him at night. It alleviates her sleeplessness and even permits her to sleep. There's a metronomic regularity to Edward's heavy breathing and his rhythmic inhalation then exhalation, as though their bed were a cradle or perhaps a sailor's hammock, and she takes pleasure in the thought that her husband, if not precisely a member of the *beati illuminati*, could qualify instead for the *beati innocenti*; he appears to have no difficulty sleeping and, as far as she can ascertain, does not have difficult dreams. She feels real consolation in his presence and believes that the comfort is mutual and has missed him these last weeks.

This continues to surprise her and it surprises her companions a great deal. She has only recently begun to take any interest in men or, as Geneviève used to claim in mock exasperation, sex at all. G. used to say that AnnaLise alone of all their circle was spiritual and did not mean it as a compliment, and often enough in the years of their friendship G. had said Oh you don't understand what you're missing and how much the body matters and how great a delight it provides; come here and I'll show you *chérie*. Often enough in the years of their friendship and in order to disprove that assertion she, AnnaLise, did go to bed with Geneviève or Linda or Roxana or Éliane. But there had never been much point to it: a kind of anxious friction, a failure to attain the celebrated orgasm, that shuddering release they spoke of with such enthusiasm, and then the wakeful sleeplessness at night. . . .

It is different with Edward, however—not the orgasm part but the sleep. They are very close, very—as the French would have it—*convenable*, and her private nickname for him is old shoe. Oh you old shoe, she likes to say, when her husband does something especially thoughtful, when he brings her still-warm croissants and jelly with the morning coffee or rubs her neck and shoulders where the tension collects at the end of the day. Hello, old shoe, she calls across the *atelier*, when she lets herself in with the groceries or when coming back from a concert alone or after a discussion with the bank officer who handles her portfolio. AnnaLise has a good deal of money and Edward a good deal of talent in spending it, and the couple are—so everyone who knows them both has if only reluctantly come to agree—well matched.

They had met three years before, at a gallery reception for American friends of the Steins. There were Avery Hop-wood and Carl Van Vechten and one of the Stettheimer sisters and photographers and sculptors and painters of every stripe and persuasion, and some of them, so Edward said, appeared to be persuaded that the coming thing was stripes. There were people wearing bowler hats and one with a waistcoat cut out of the same material as his bow tie and one man with a lobster on a leash. The lobster was dying, or dead. You couldn't tell, because it bumped and scuttled along the floor in any case, but it couldn't be good for a lobster to be so far from salt water and dragged around the gallery floor at the end of a red leather leash. There were many crit-ics and collectors and she, AnnaLise, was wondering just how long she would be expected to stay and when it would be possible to leave.

Then this tall boy with a scraggly beard he was attempt-ing to cultivate said, Look at that, and pointed to identical haystacks done in six different versions of light. It was an homage to Monet, of course, and she had tried to tell him so, but none of this impressed him; he said, Don't think I'm impressed by Monet. What he had been admiring, he told her, was the pitchfork and the pair of rubber boots at the top right quadrant of the canvas, and this was so perverse a form of admiration that she looked at her companion to see if he was being serious. He was. He had done a lot of haying in his time, he told her, too much haying, too many summers of haying, and what he really liked was the way the farm-hand you can't see in the picture but who—judging from the sun's position in the top right panel—must be on his lunchtime break and lying invisibly on the far side of the haystack had taken off his boots.

They went to a café. It had been Le Select, or Dôme, or maybe the Brasserie Lipp. So you're a painter? she inquired, and he said, No, I'm not. A collector then, she asked him, or a photographer; which? I'm not, he said again. Three strikes I'm out, said AnnaLise, and then he explained he was a writer and she wanted to respond, but did not, oh what a disappointment oh dear me. If there's anything worse I don't know it, a *writer*: always ready with a bright remark, always *reading* a picture, explaining things, always assum-ing the world's built of words. So she drained her glass and Edward must have noticed how she was losing interest, how he'd lost her claim on his attention but then he said, At least I'm not a critic and she said, Yes, I grant you that much, that's true. So they walked together by the Seine, and he knew a surprising amount of Verlaine, and his French was surprisingly good.

One month later they were married, and they have been married three years. It surprises AnnaLise still, a little, that she should have taken a husband, and it surprised and grieved others considerably. How could you do this? Geneviève asked. What are you even *thinking* about; what sort of *folie* have you embarked on, my friend? It had caused a small rupture between them, but then G. started crying and said, Pay me no attention, oh, don't pay me any atten-tion, I just want you to be happy and not to suffer, ever. If it makes you happy, puss, why then I'm happy too. . . .

She had had a pet when young, a brown curly retriever called Gus. Her father was a sportsman, and he said that curly retrievers have a great gift of retrieval and can swim underwater for great distances. But it became apparent to his handlers that Gus was a failure as bird dog; Who ever heard of a bird dog, they asked, that doesn't care to swim? On the occasion of her sixth birthday, therefore, her father removed Gus from the kennels and said, He just wants to lie around and lollygag, he isn't adequate at being a retriever and from now on he's your pet.

Whatever his shortcomings in the field and underwater, as a house dog Gus—the name had been shortened from Gusto—was beyond reproach; he lay at the foot of her bed every night; he ran by her side when she went out bicycling or waited at the kitchen door for her to return home from school. He had been faithful and intelligent and focused, and though she would not ever dream of saying this to Edward, or Geneviève, or anyone, what she liked about having a husband was what, so many years before, she had liked about having a dog. The rewards were not dissimilar: the mutual attentiveness and reciprocated need. It was the kind of creature comfort one creature can offer another, and AnnaLise felt grateful, daily, that she had taken him in.

So Edward moved into her lodgings, her high-ceilinged many-windowed flat overlooking the Seine, and she enjoyed supporting him and watching while he wrote. She would curl up in the easy chair with a *café au lait* or glass of white wine, and she would have a book to read or magazine to look at or perhaps a scarf or shawl to keep her fingers occupied, because she still did like to knit and could do so without thinking, and she'd let herself daydream and drift.

At such times she thought about her family, her parents in Old Saybrook and the white eighteenth-century clapboard farmhouse they adored and had been restoring for years. She thought about her brother, his earnest pursuit of possessions, his brokerage firm and unhappy marriage and how long it would last before his new wife procured a settlement and moved back to Los Angeles with her leather fetish and her assortment of jewels. Her sister-in-law Katya was one of those society ladies who appear often in photographs, sporting an expansive smile and an expensive neck-

lace and a glass of champagne, at some sort of charity function in a magazine or on the rear sheets of a newspaper,
and she had a collection of tooled leather boots and was
certainly no one's old shoe. AnnaLise would knit and rumi-
nate about the members of her family and how long it had
been since she herself had lived in America, and the difference in her own case between exile and expatriation. The
former was involuntary and the latter voluntary, the former a choice made by others and the latter a choice that
you make for yourself. To begin with the whole continent
of Australia had been populated by convicts, except of
course for all those aborigines that the convicts in their
own turn slaughtered and confined. There were political
refugees, of course, and refugees of conscience and dispos-
sessed peasants and pilgrims and conscripts, and everyone
in exile is in exile for a reason, but each of the expatriates
believes in their freedom of choice.

This was the sort of topic she thought about while knit-
ting. The issue of neutrality and how to deal with borders,
the way her friend Nicole with the walled garden simply
disappeared one day, the whole question of her brother and
Katya or trains and Mussolini or engines and Marinetti
could keep her up at night before but now no longer had the
power to compel her into wakefulness while she attempted
sleep. Now she lay down beside Edward and arranged her
breathing to coincide with his and, surprisingly, gratefully,
slept.

AnnaLise adds a thin slice of lemon to her *infusion* and
stares out the dining car window. *Schatz* had wanted her to
take a plane, but the weather was unsettled and she was not
adventurous and did not like to fly. It is fine to be making
this journey by train—the light so brilliant on the hills, the
Lombardy poplars and plane trees and pines—and to be
going down to Switzerland for a period of rest. In their village, she is certain, there will be no hysterics about expatriation or the healthful effects of an orgasm and no one will

be walking with a lobster on a leash. She has left all that behind.

Instead she allows herself now to driftingly think about Edward, how he stands so straight while writing, favoring his back. He had wrenched it badly and the doctors said there might be curvature or a compression of the discs or some sort of degeneration of the spine and it hurt him less to stand. Poor darling, he was terrified and tried very hard not to show it, and when she said, Let's go to Switzerland and have a little landscape, he was grateful in that way of his he tried very hard not to show. She said, It will be good for us, it will be fine to get some air, and then she told him, Go ahead and find us a place to your liking and I'll join you when you're good and ready as soon as I close up the flat. Do you mean it? he had asked her, and she said, Of course, old shoe.

That had been five weeks ago. He wrote and telephoned and said he hoped she would feel travelly and take a plane or, if she preferred it, a train; then he telegrammed he had found them a house with a view of the Alps, she should hurry to join him and see. Do bring along my stories, won't you? Edward asked her on the telephone, and she asked him to tell her which stories, and where they had been stored. He explained that he kept all his drafts and carbons in a suitcase, the one in the hall closet, and that he chucked his work there every day for safekeeping; his preference, he said, was always for the wastebasket but it was an impulse to guard against, his habitual confusion of baby with bathwater, for the suitcase was a bathtub in which baby need not drown. Or, to alter and improve the figure, a receptacle from which his old abandoned work could be retrieved.

He wasn't all that serious about his writing, really; it was an occupation like others he had tried. He had hobbies too, of course, and many other interests and forms of occupation. It had been bullfights the first year and racing the year after that. He liked to go out to Enghien or to the track at Auteuil and handicap the horses and compute what would have happened if he had placed a wager; then, when she furnished an allowance, he liked to place bets and win. More often than not, naturally, Edward lost, but since it was her money and she made him a *cadeau* of it he did not seem to mind. Then, when he reached his betting limit on the horses and wanted to place bets instead on the Tour de France, she assisted him with that. He learned a great deal, with celerity, about contestants in the Tour de France, and whom to bet on and what obstacles they faced. He became an expert, and the touts that he brought back with him for pastis and handicapping all told her how much of an expert their new friend her husband was. His favorite broke an ankle on the third day out, however, so that also proved a failure, and now once again his pastime was writing; now what he did was compose.

This was comparatively inexpensive, and AnnaLise encouraged it; he wrote after breakfast each day. He liked to stand at the Louis XVI desk, favoring his back and doing exercises for his spine and writing, in his small precise hand, with pencils he sharpened continually. This was his abiding interest, after all; it was what he'd claimed to do that first night at the Gallery and by the river when quoting Verlaine. So she had been pleased to fulfill his request; she found the suitcase where he'd said she would and had the concierge deposit it in the taxi for the Gare de Lyon and carried his stories along.

He is standing on the platform, looking well. Edward has put on weight, a little, and his Alpine jacket bulks out at the waist, but his expression is cheerful and expectant and already he seems to stand straighter; this must be, she tells herself, what they mean by *bracing* air. He has been smoking with the porter, and there's a dog—part shepherd and part something nondescript—lying at his heels. The weeks in the country have helped his complexion, and his knitted cap is optimistic, and the station smells of chocolate and firewood and sawdust; there's a kiosk for bratwurst and beer. He takes her hand in that enveloping familiar grasp of his, and then she offers him her cheek—first the right cheek, then the left—and they embrace.

Was the journey pleasant? *Schatz* inquires, and she tells him yes.

Did you have difficulty sleeping? and she tells him no.

The train whistle sounds. The train leaves. There's the rumble and clatter of steel on the tracks, the great iron symphony shaping its sound. *Crescendo, forte, fortissimo, diminuendo, ralentando, piano, pianissimo,* repeat. (Questions: Is she musical? Is he? Do we have to establish that *leitmotif* more clearly and does the reader care? Could we accomplish in sonorous terms what was earlier attempted in relation to canvas and film, so that the word "compose" refers to music equally?) For now, from somewhere off stage left, or in the rear chair of the orchestra, sounds a single note she hears and turns her head to try to identify, but cannot quite place in terms of either location or source: What are we hearing? she asks.

Her Edward smiles his smile. He knows; he's been waiting to tell her; he's fairly bursting with pleasure at the prearranged surprise. They have made you some music, he says. It's the custom of the country, here, to greet a new arrival and arrange a serenade.

Yes, but with what instrument?

Ah, *that,* he says, that's the surprise.

Then he speaks about the Swiss horn, its complexity and beauty and its function in these mountains. He tells her the sound is both plaintive and fierce, a musical echo from peak to peak, and he describes the shape and construction of the instrument and its characteristic timbre and sonority with such precision and specific knowledge of the difficulties entailed that AnnaLise knows his affections once again have shifted and that he now desires and expects to be a musician. When she asks him does he practice he says yes. For hours every day, he says; I'll play you *Frère Jacques* and *Auprès de ma blonde.* When she asks him has he found a horn that suits his present fancy he smiles that boyish smile of his and, confirming her guess, bobs his head. I bought myself one, he admits.

So when they start to leave and she recollects the suitcase it is not that awful, really. She claps her hand to her mouth and says, Oh, Edward, *que je suis idiote*, I left your suitcase in the train, I was sitting in the dining car and, darling, I simply forgot. What an idiot I've been and what a perfect fool I am and do you hate me? He says no. Do you forgive me? He says yes.

The question of complicity will occupy her later; later she will wonder to what degree she had been conscious in this gesture of abandonment, if she even *remembered* the suitcase, forgot to take it off the train or if the promptings of her own unconscious—so she would ask her doctors in the future, in Scarsdale and Old Saybrook and Manhattan when her brother was divorced at last and she and G. were reconciled—had simply been too strong.

Coda. Passacaglia. Fugue.

But Edward had been masterful; he mastered himself and squared his shoulders and took a deep breath and, after an instant, could manage a smile.

It doesn't matter, he declares, I was planning to dispense with them and throw them out in any case; I'm better now, much better really, and it would be embarrassing to read those stories now. I have put away, says Edward, childish things.

Or picture it this way:

She gets off the train.

She has been carrying his suitcase, has watched it ceaselessly and borne and *presided* over it as might a priestess or a vestal maiden, as though it were an object of collective veneration and inestimable value, as though what he entrusted to her is the very pith and marrow of his future, therefore theirs. Her name is AnnaLise. She loves him, this month, very much. He has swept her off her feet. That she has been so elevated with some regularity is beside the present point;

like a heroine in Ovid she renews herself while airborne and reconstitutes virginity by just such a lightsome leap. A stewardess, perhaps? A transatlantic sweetheart with a boyfriend in each port?

Her mother, Elizabeth, was born in Hamburg and her father, Hans, in Berlin. But her parents have long since departed Germany, first moving to Brazil and then America in order to pursue what her father called the obvious advantages of commerce here, the triumphant refutation of that tract he so despises, *Das Kapital*, the odious and self-evidently inaccurate prediction of Karl Marx and his even more mistaken mentor, Friedrich Engels. And then taking advantage of, as who would not, the business opportunities and the import-export license he had obtained for paintbrushes, hair brushes, nail brushes, toothbrushes, stockpiling in his warehouse on the south side of Chicago the supple Chinese bristles from the nape of the pig's neck, and kollinsky, and Chunking two-three-quarter, and profiting, as who would not, from well-advised and cautious speculation in the stock exchange and commodity futures and watching with earned gratification as his portfolio increased in value, doubling then quadrupling and then continuing to increase exponentially before the crash. And in this version of the tale, this attempt to justify A's name and nationality, the winters in Winnetka grow—though this is only how they *feel* and not, of course, statistically the case—colder and more lengthy and an insult to aging bones. Why should we not and can we not relieve ourselves a little, Hans, and have we not deserved it, and why must we remain as though imprisoned in the jail of this chill northern place? And if we do linger here all winter then I am obliged to inquire, *Schatz*, why did we bother leaving Hamburg in the first place, or Berlin? For it is cold in Illinois and as dark as in the Schwarzwald's depths or the wind-whipped black sands above Bremen; it is insupportable. And therefore on her dentist's good advice one afternoon after her bridgework and a filling in the right bicuspid Elizabeth and Hans elect instead the milder clime of Florida,

where they and others of their class will purchase what are
called vacation homes along the gulf—intending them at
first as winter cottages, a place for fish and a game perhaps
of tennis and then bingo and bridge and relaxation, and little by little discover that the beneficent effects of sun are, as
Marx would no doubt have understood had he not chained
himself to that hard stool in the British Museum Reading
Room, the opiate of the people, the consolations of philoso-
phy and flesh.

Ach, Karl, you sharpen your pencil too much.

Ach, Friedrich, come down here and look.

She is the child of their old age. AnnaLise is their blessing
and prize. Since the moment of their transatlantic relocation,
again without discussing it, they have decided they would
prove unable to have children. They have not gone to doctors
or for tests but have thought themselves too old, and ill, and
therefore when one morning Elizabeth felt dizzy and *übel*,
when she developed an insupportable craving for chocolate
and pickles and grapes, they did not understand that this
would be a prayer answered, a cornucopia of gladnesses, a bun
in the oven, laughs Hans. She has been named for his aunt.
Her eyes are an untroubled azure and her curls are red. She is
delightful, charming, so good with her letters and music and
so polite to visitors, *entzückend*, good enough to eat. They
dote upon her, both of them; they spoil their *liebchen* shamelessly because you cannot love a child too much and there will
surely be trouble enough in the future in this vale of tears
and whatever we do to postpone it is a parental kindness and
a thing we ought to do. And although we two may suffer disagreements and the occasional quarrel as to which car to purchase or what color to paint the pantry or which candidate to
vote for for mayor we are of the same opinion here, completely in agreement, a child cannot be spoiled. For, as it does
not take a Sophocles to tell us, man's fate is pain, loss, grief.

But in the meantime there is soup to drink and wine to
cultivate a taste for and tennis and piano lessons to pay for
and foreign languages to acquire and ballet class and swim-

ming and dancing instruction at Miss Porterfield's and dolphins to watch at their leisurely sport. Hans and Elizabeth have come to occupy this structure on Mexico's Gulf, the house they bought in 19—, and here they sit and smoke their meerschaum pipe and cigarettes and play nine holes of golf together and sometimes eighteen and improve a little on the handicap and learn when which iron is suitable where and admire the hibiscus and the gong-tormented sea foam. We want nothing so much for ourselves any longer, but only that our daughter will be happy, will not suffer, and therefore in the course of things when she comes home and steps down from the train and on the platform announces that she plans to marry a fine upright boy from Oak Park and a doctor's family it doesn't seem so bad. He is, of course, not Jewish but in this enlightened day and age it matters less than you might think, it's a matter of preference mostly. Oh daddy I love him so much. Oh mummy have you ever felt the way I feel today? He is working for a newspaper, he wants to be a writer, and according to their daughter, though of course she is bedazzled, he is very well respected already in his chosen profession and talented and brave.

Is she pregnant; if so, does she know? If she carries a child, is it his?

The reader will have noticed, *certes*, that what we have here is again a variation on a theme. But how many *are* there, after all, how much is superfluity, too much of a good thing? And questions may arise once more as to the temporal sequence; when does this action transpire precisely, and precisely where? Are they themselves Jewish or simply prescient and in any event suspicious of the Kaiser; does this antedate the crash? Which one? Will Hans the aging immigrant (exile? refugee? the soon-to-be displaced executive of a Berlin-based import-export firm?) retain his warehouses and real estate and stock market fortune and, if not, how much does he lose? Does this in any way impinge upon or alter the affections of that seemingly disinterested artist who courted their treasure, their pearl beyond price? And what of that leashed lobster and the homage to Monet? For now that there is nothing here to keep them both, no tangled web to weave or filament of vows or braided set of parental expectations to honor because they are after all married and empowered to depart, with their papers in order, their letters of introduction and credit, their promises to write home often and their Mont Blanc or is it Jungfrau pens and sufficient supply of French letters, his heaving bulk imprinted on the white sheet of her body, her scrawled endearments everywhere, his tongue ubiquitous, untramelled, and now that they abandon us we two cannot follow and even supposing we did choose to follow we would not of course be welcome where they post with such hot haste. And is it not ironic, is it not the case that we might find this risible or in any case a *narrheit* that we who crossed the ocean in pursuit of liberty must arrive at this point to discover that our daughter does likewise except in the other direction? How can they go together where we swore we would not stay? Have they learned nothing from our history and are they therefore doomed to repeat it? Has the Old World debauched the New, or vice versa, or both?

Thirteen more ways of looking at a suitcase:

1. Glancingly.
2. Closely.
3. Assessingly, alertly. As part of a uniform set: three matched pieces, maybe five. Has this particular one been opened, slashed, rifled, tampered with, discolored, or replaced? Will we file a claim or lodge a complaint with our insurance agent as soon as we get back? Did we keep and can we locate proof of purchase in 19—?
4. Wearily. What a sonofabitching trip. You wouldn't believe it. The weather. The fuck-ups in Denver, then Minneapolis, the goddamn cancellations, and then the goddamn lines.

5. Enviously. This battered well-worn expensively tooled leather and the scurf of usage and array of far-flung labels argues—to the noticing eye—distant adventures undertaken and places seen and been and challenges met and surmounted and stories to tell and then write.

6. Identifyingly. While waiting, say, to claim same on the ground floor of Detroit Metro at baggage conveyor belt #3.

7. Proudly. Mom, Dad, I made it, I'm home.

8. Happily. Heigh-ho, heigh-ho, it's off to school we go.

9. Anxiously. *Must* I; do I *have* to?

10. Repeatedly. Is it time to replace this old bag of a bag, how long have I owned it, how long will it last?

11. Repeatedly. My *fides Achates* and faithful companion, my whither thou goest I go.

12. Suspiciously. How much can it carry, how much will it weigh? Whose fingerprint is that? Who attempted when to force the lock, and did he or she succeed? Where's the key? Who spilled what looks like brandy on the corner reinforcement patch and who were you with, you bastard, in that hotel in Biarritz?

13. Imploringly. Oh please oh please please don't be lost.

THREE

Or perhaps our AnnaLise is angry, enraged at what her husband said or failed to say, and therefore deciding to wound him and wondering what would hurt most. Their marriage is over, she knows. It is only a question of which of them ends it, and in what manner and when; there are many ways to do so, and she asks herself how to proceed. She wants to be the one to leave and not the one he leaves. It is, she thinks, enough, or maybe what she means is not enough. They have argued noisily and silently and lengthily and abruptly; it is, she tells herself, too much, or maybe the word is too little.

Last night again E. returned to the flat at three o'clock in the morning and took a shower immediately, then came to bed, his hair still wet, smelling of soap and not-washed-away sex, but lying beside her so placid, so spent, that self-satisfied half smile all over his face. In the morning he explains that he's been working on a story about night-soil carts and the last of the men in their part of the city who labor till dawn in the morgue or cart off dead bodies to Père Lachaise. Of course he must scrub off the germs. It's a clever explanation, for she shrinks from him and has no wish to touch him on arrival, and his notebook does bristle with jargon that he learned in l'Abbatoir. But AnnaLise has long ago discovered his repeated infidelities, which she is certain are actual although he tells her they're imagined. And although this is that time of month when she does get imaginative and does invent things sometimes or, as he tells her, does overreact, she feels she simply has to puncture, *prick* the enormous balloon of his vanity, the vast blimp of E's self-regard. It has been inflated too much. It is, she wants to tell him, overweening and excessive and absurd.

Her husband has only two passions: the first for his reflection in a mirror and the second for the prospect of his titles on a shelf. Edward lies there, having showered, having thrown his clothes into the hamper, and reeking of cologne. He pretends to be asleep. So every night for a fortnight AnnaLise has pretended it also, lying by his side in bed, adjusting her breathing to his. In perfect hypocrisy they lie there together while she asks herself how best to wound him and he replays his conquest of the evening in his head.

It has happened before, happened often before, first when he started playing cards and then when he went to the races in order to complete what he described as research and then when he went to the bullfights and later on to Africa and came back from the wars. He was covered in glory and medals, at least according to the dispatches he wrote about his exploits, except all he did was write stories and she sometimes wondered if indeed he ever went to Turkey or to Africa. Perhaps all he did for heroics was visit a bar in some part of the city she herself does not frequent and meet a girl from Aquila or Constantinople or Nairobi and go upstairs and pay for whatever she offered and listen to her tale of woe and then write it down. Or he bought a round of drinks for soldiers, for *condottieri* or some one-armed major back from the front who was wearing bandages and had in truth seen action on the Bosporus or at Khartoum, and then he copied place names and the names of regiments and sent a telegram.

To begin with it had been comic and even a little endearing: how each fight he fought entailed three, five, *eleven* men, how every trout he caught or every buck he shot was record-breaking in its size and every book he planned to write was better than Turgenev. And what she had noticed to start with, the first time she had slept with him in the room among the fir trees in the hunting camp, and then when he proposed to her and then on the otherwise-pleasant-enough honeymoon and then all through the early months of their marriage and deciding to settle in Paris was his little-boy anxiety, his at-first-endearing hunger for her compliments, Oh, darling, you're the best that ever was, the best that ever could be, oh absolutely the best.

To begin with he believed her, or appeared to, accepting that there never was or could ever be any other man so manly or lover so splendid, a writer so gifted and husband so fine. And it had not been difficult; she more than half-meant what she whispered and almost half-meant what she said. For there had been a transparency to his lying and his neediness that AnnaLise found touching and even, a little, enjoyed. It reminded her of childhood, when she needed her father to come to the room and shine his flashlight under her bed and assure her that there was no danger, promising her he was just down the hall and could hear her at once if she woke in the night and there were no gorillas, never any tigers to bother her or spider bats in their part of the world. She should close her eyes, her father said, and no harm would ever come to her or happen in the house. And although AnnaLise knew he was lying or at least not telling the whole truth there'd been comfort in the ritual: his way of bending from the waist, his Eveready flashlight and the wax on his still-black moustache.

But for a long time lately it has not been enjoyable: E's boastfulness, his self-inflating storytelling and inventiveness about the war that has been growing worse and worse and is no doubt connected to rum. Or beer with a whiskey chaser and vermouth and tequila and gin. Or Campari and vodka and Pernod and Fernet-Branca and wine. Or perhaps he has inherited his family's propensity to madness and then suicide; perhaps the melancholy has descended from those ancestors who killed themselves and from the package that his mother sent, which revealed, when he unwrapped it, his father's suicide gun. But whatever the cause of the problem it is no longer pleasant, it means breast-beating and chest-pounding and masculine boasting and is almost entirely false.

Over the years she exhausted herself with the effort to bolster his ego, for his need was inexhaustible; there were only so many forms of flattery, only so many ways to assure or reassure him, and he had been insatiable for praise. He could not get enough of it; he took and took and took. In the bottomless reflecting pool of his self-absorption and his vanity every other writer was a rival and every critic a fool. Unless, that is, the critics praised him, in which case they were intelligent but stupid in their choice of a career. The world was Edward's mirror, as AnnaLise had come to see, and the only face he studied or admired was his own. So when finally she wearied of falsehood and began to need to tell him the truth or at least not continue with lying in bed, he had turned for consolation elsewhere, she was certain, to those who would praise him instead.

Well, let them try. Let them exhaust themselves with flattery until they too were sick of it and would be replaced. For this explained the coat-check girl at the Crillon and Madame Helvetius's niece the aspiring actress and that war correspondent with the legs she insisted on crossing and uncrossing on the couch. And this explained Nurse Agnes with her uniform and blonde hair in a bun and the hairpins that AnnaLise found in his shirt. . . .

I'm going, E. declared. I need some time in the country. I require time alone.

Alone? she asked. Don't you mean what you need is to be there without me?

All right, he admitted, if that's the way you want to put it.

And who's the lucky lady? AnnaLise had asked.

What do you mean? E. inquired. What are you trying to say?

You'll be there, won't you, she had said, with company while you're alone. With someone else to shine the mirror and change the water in the pool.

Why don't you come along, he asked, not meaning it, and when she said, No thank you, no, he looked less disappointed than relieved. Well, if you change your mind, he offered, I'll write with an address as soon as I get one, and she said, Yes, tell me how it goes. I do need to forward your mail.

Oh, let it go. Leave it alone. Let this sleeping dog lie and this lying dog sleep while she ponders the shape of revenge. It is surely, *ja, certo*, her turn. She has hurt him in small ways often before, as he with his unfaithfulness and callow disregard has wounded her. He has offended and assaulted her, although not with his hands. But there are other methods of assault, and he has caused her to suffer greatly and now no longer has that power and it is her turn. She had been precious to him once, as these drafts and stories are precious to him still, and she will be the engine of destruction so he in turn may understand how it feels to be destroyed.

(N.B. The reader will now note, no doubt, that in this version of the story we deal with conscious volition. AnnaLise intends to make the stories disappear, she wants them and the suitcase lost: no inadvertence here.)

Therefore on Tuesday morning when E. sets off for Switzerland, first stopping at the office in order, he says, to file the graveyard piece but really, she is certain, to arrange an assignation with the new layout editor, AnnaLise takes his short stories, his drafts for a novel, and his fair copies and carbons. Next she selects a brown valise and places the papers inside. She scours the apartment for all traces of his prose and also the love poems that he sent her early on, the ones where he compared her to an unexpected snowfall in late springtime and to a fly in a trout stream and then the mountain wind. Once he called her his gazelle and once an antelope, and she had taken that as praise until she came to understand how animals were things he killed and skinned or stuffed.

E. is on the way to Switzerland, on the way out of her life. He does not know it yet, of course, because all he knows and admires and writes about is what he sees in the mirror. She has forgiven him often before, and has attempted to forget and even at times succeeded in forgetting how often he betrayed her. When a bone is broken it can be set; when it breaks again it may heal repeatedly, but over time the resistance wears out and all the resilience wears down. Perhaps Nurse Agnes understands the way to set a broken bone, perhaps she's the one he requires to soothe his broken ego and heal his broken heart. . . .

This is one of those mornings the city feels clean, when the rain has sluiced down the gutters and everything gleams as though innocent, freshly: a first hint of heat in the air. She could just deposit the container and the tales contained in one of the trash baskets on the Rue Cardinal Lemoine or in a cart full of dung. She could pursue the men with night-soil carts he has cultivated lately and say, *Tiens,* you know my husband, would you give this to him please? She could hand it to a beggar or policeman or throw the thing into the Seine.

It might, however, float. Or the beggar might be disappointed in his hope of redeemable value or the *flic* might attempt to identify and then return the suitcase to its owner or, in the Seine, it might be buffeted toward the bank or fished out of the water by a tourist or a fisherman who believes he's hooked something to eat. And since AnnaLise must dispose of the suitcase past all possibility of retrieval, she decides on the Gare de Lyon. She will drop it in the dustman's bin for unclaimed or unwanted possessions, the torn shirts and used newspaper and half-eaten sandwiches and broken umbrellas: the wreckage and detritus left behind at journeys' end.

A spring in her stride.

A jauntiness. A cleansing rush of fury and the rightness in revenge:

This is for Agnes and the layout editor and the Helvetius niece. *This* for the war correspondent you thought was so brave and *this* for the whore in the Pera Palas you wrote of so pantingly, pillows and all. This one's for Martha and that one for Mary and this is for Pauline. Now each of the versions you pulled off so pridefully are languishing here in the Gare de Lyon; each of the women is *written*, my dear, and every last one of them lost.

Thirteen ways of hiding a suitcase:

1. Under the bed.
2. In the back of the master bedroom closet, behind the stacked shoeboxes on the second shelf.
3. In the attic, near the blanket chest, underneath the hammock you bought in the Andes and slept in all through that dangerous summer and the clothing bags with camphor and the scarves and caps and mittens and sweaters stored against the coming fall—though it's hot up here, so hot up here you can't remember or imagine that you ever were or ever again could be cold.

4. In the basement. Near the furnace and the broken water heater and the litterbox left for the cat.

5. From your wife. Because it signifies your willingness to leave, your readiness at any moment for departure and the cessation of hostilities your going will entail.

6. From your biographers. Who want to know what you had for breakfast on the first Monday morning in June in 1922, and at what hour breakfast was served, and by whom, and who joined you at the table, and what they were wearing, and the name of the headwaiter at the restaurant you chose for lunch and what the weather forecast was that day of the fiesta, and whether in fact it did rain. Who want to know the name of the book you were reading, which books were on the hotel shelf and in which editions, and want to know so that they may in tedious detail report upon the tedious details of your writing habits, the locality of purchase and the brand and price of the pencils and pens you deploy and in the former instance how often you hand-sharpen them and in the latter instance the variety of ink. Who plan to list the birthdate of your first grade teacher and the middle name of the one who taught you penmanship in third grade, and list the seven mispelled (misspeled?) words in your first published short story, and whether you preferred Lou Gehrig to Babe Ruth that season, and whether you prefer peas to beans and argyle socks to black or white. But who know nothing at all, nothing even remotely about your real imagined life.

7. From yourself. From an instinct and impulse—obscure but decisive—that says it's better left alone, better left unpublished against the rainy future day when perhaps you're less productive and can pull memories out of this suitcase-hat.

8. With the family silver, and banknotes in stacks, and the Rembrandt drawing of a man with a cap and his chin on his hands and the letter that the Queen of Sweden wrote great-great-great uncle Abraham announcing she would visit on her journey south from Uppsala, and the diamond necklace and ear-rings that grandfather presented to his bride as an engagement gift: these wrapped into a prayer shawl and stuffed into the suitcase and buried beneath the linden tree in the rear garden by the rosebush-es where we devoutly hope the Gestapo will be too busy to look and where when things get back to normal in this *verdammte* country perhaps we can dig the bag up.

9. From the police.

10. From your creditors. Detractors. Your editor and agent and money-grubbing cousin and shark of a first wife.

11. So that at some time and place unimaginable to you from your present vantage those who follow in your footsteps will unearth it by conscious inten-tion or perhaps a happy accident and turn to each other wonderingly and with a wild surmise ask, *tiens*, what have we here?

12. Amateurishly. With branches that scatter and leaves that blow off and earth that bears the mark of spadework or in a culvert that will empty out with the first rushing torrents of spring.

13. Professionally. Deeper than did ever plummet sound I'll drown my book.

As suggested above, Edward drinks. He does this with a con-trolled abandon that AnnaLise at first believed in but now understands has controlled him instead. To begin with she thought it amusing, a sociable hilarity, a form of play when work was done and something he could choose to do or not. And it had been romantic, a form of adventure and fun. At first she joined him, drinking, and one of the things he admired, he said, was how well she could hold her drink and how rarely she got tight. I mean this as a compliment, he told her: you don't drink like a woman you drink just like a man. Except there was no limit to his drinking and AnnaLise had limits; admittedly her limits were extensive, but she did know when to stop.

There was wine at lunch and wine in the *bota* he carried when they walked or went out fishing and bottles cached in trees and set to cool in streams. There were martinis and mint juleps and something called a Black Russian and mixed drinks called Sidecars or Singapore Slings. There was beer in the afternoon and sometimes in the early morning to keep the edge honed while he worked and then single-malt scotch whiskey before a siesta and gin and rum and rye and, when he returned from Mexico, tequila for cocktails and wine again for dinner, with perhaps a grappa or single malt whiskey once more or brandy or a poire or pruneau afterward. And although she had a good stomach and head she could not entirely keep pace with him, and did not want to anyhow; she lost count of the bottles by dinner if they had visitors or went to someone else's house or out to a bistro or restaurant where someone of the party knew the owner or the bartender or made friends with other customers while E. continued roaring, drinking, trading punches with his windmills in the night.

That was what he called them: windmills, the big-bladed paddles that turn while you sleep, the things you must attempt to keep at bay with rum. I come from La Mancha, he liked to declare, I've had my battle of Lepanto and been imprisoned afterward and I tell you there are windmills and they need to be harnessed and tilted with, Daughter; they have to be defeated by your knight without reproach.

Come off it, *Schatz*, she tried to say. We don't have any daughters and even if we did I'm not your daughter but wife. You're not a knight-errant or *preux chevalier*, you're just a no-longer-quite-so-attractive falling-down drunk and country boy besotted by the grape. That's it, he said, that's what you think, is that what you think, Dulcinea? My name's not Dulcinea, she reminded him, less cheerfully, hearing the grandfather clock in the hall, and you're not Don Quixote and it's time to get some sleep. Windmills, he told her, that's what they are, this is excellent and dulcet brandy but now I'll lay me down with you and try to get some sleep.

Too, in this draft they have a son, and he is three years old by now and promises to be as active and boisterous as his father, and as difficult to placate or control. All day long he rackets around with the neighborhood boys and *la nourrice* on the *rez de chaussée*, but by supper he comes home again and she has her hands full once more. At night their son Bumpy—his real name isn't Bumpy, of course, but he gave himself that nickname by crowing delightedly, clapping his hands while he bumped down the high central stairwell of her parents' summer house last August, on their annual visit, and the nickname stuck—has difficulty sleeping, and he still wets the bed on occasion during a bad dream. She loves him to distraction, and would not change him for the world, but "bumpy" is the word for how she feels about the world these days, and it doesn't help to have a son who likes to suck on shotgun shells his father leaves behind. Or who wants to practice tying flies with safety pins as hooks. For she is pregnant with their second child, and there is something more than usually dispiriting about a man who sleeps with your best friend while you are pregnant and calls you "Daughter" meanwhile as a sign of affection; the man who properly should call her daughter is living in America and far too far away.

Nonetheless she tries. Lord knows and as God is her witness and as her friends will in divorce court attest our AnnaLise has tried. On Bumpy's third birthday she baked him a cake and invited everybody they knew, or cared to know, in Paris. It was quite the affair. There were balloons and acrobats and a waiter from the restaurant across the street who wanted to be a magician and several musicians with trumpets and drums and guitars. There were children from the playschool and their parents and chauffeurs. The flat was small and airless and it had not been easy to invite so many people to it, or imagine them mingling and breathing the air, but E. said, What the hell, we have only one Mr. Bumpy and he will have only one third birthday party and what the hell, Daughter, let's give it a try.

The pregnancy was difficult. AnnaLise had many headaches and much morning sickness and a continual desire to lie undisturbed in bed. When she carried Mr. Bumpy the pregnancy had been, by comparison, simple, so little a problem she barely had noticed and went skiing and swimming for months. But ever since their son arrived she seems to have less energy or is the proper word resilience; she is, as Doctor Diver warned her, running down.

I'm not a wristwatch, she reminded him, not something to wind up. Of course not, said the doctor, but you must conserve your energy, you mustn't feel you have to do everything, or do it all by yourself.

Nevertheless she shopped and cooked and prepared the table festively, and there were rabbits and a kitten called F. Puss the waiter promised to pull out of hats. But all that week she had had a foreboding, a feeling that this birthday would be the last of many fêtes. When she woke with the windows open and the moonlight on the roofs of the tall houses, it was there. She put her face away from the moonlight into the shadow but could not sleep and lay awake thinking about it. For E. had discovered a deadline again, and had become exuberantly busy at the office with what she knew was the new secretary but what he claimed was just an article he had been asked to deliver on that season's Tour de France.

When she reproached him—not with the long-legged stenographer or the layout editor but with his absence from the fête—he said, Yes, I know, but how do you think we can pay for the cake or all those rabbits and F. Puss otherwise. I'll arrive at the party in good time, I promise, and I'll bring the wine. She had had no choice, of course; when you're pregnant and giving a party you rely on the kindness of husbands to assist with the arrangements; you yourself are too distracted to consider his distractedness and absence from the house. Or what he thinks of you this first trimester, with your headaches and swollen ankles and bad breath. Or how he's been avoiding you, and who has been his glad companion in avoidance every night. Avoidance has grown pervasive, not to say repetitive, for even these last sentences and their organizing syntax submit to such circumlocution, and the forward motion of our tale has proved digressive instead. But to be fair about it E. did arrive, his arms full of bottles, his pockets stuffed with the double-*graisse* chèvre wrapped in grape leaves, his moustache freshly trimmed and his laughter infectious, as always, and so everyone was glad to see him and said how well he looked and how fine a father he was.

At five o'clock, as the party began, AnnaLise felt her headache come on. It was like a giant hand pressing down upon her temples, or a set of pliers, or somebody grinding an axe. She had had the nausea all day long but was determined to be festive, and she tried very hard to continue but could not manage it.

Then their great friend Pauline appeared, wearing the tight silk dress that was modeled on the Japanese kimono and had been all the rage in Paris that spring, and took stock of the situation and declared, Of course you must let me arrange it, of course you must lie down. The best thing to do is do nothing and use this cold compress, then hot. I'll come in and change the compress every half hour, I promise; now *your* job is only to rest.

She had been grateful and relieved to let Pauline play hostess and welcome all their guests. From her room in the back of the flat she could hear the singing and the laughter and the sound of glasses clinking and the way the company sang "Happy birthday, Bumpy," loudly, uproariously. Then E. sang, "For he's a jolly good fellow" all by himself, off-key. She had never guessed—or if she guessed had told herself not to be silly, it was the headache talking and the suspicions of a pregnant woman who would otherwise not be suspicious—that E. and Pauline had been seeing each other, that she had set her cap for him and he had been, of course, of course, receptive. Pauline was lonely, rich, and bored, and when she took Bumpy to the Tuileries last Saturday he came back with ice cream and a toy boat with a set of sails and when she met E. at Michaud's for Tuesday lunch they played footsie and boot-sie and tootsie under the table together. She should have guessed, of course, of course, but failed to see the signs.

The party had been a success. At nine o'clock the guests dispersed and came two by two to the foot of her bed and said what a fine time they had and hoped she would feel bet-ter soon, and then they said good-bye. Then when the fête was finally over and AnnaLise could try to rest the two of them arrived together and were the picture of solicitude and changed the compress over her eyes—first warm, then cold, then warm again—until she fell asleep at last, with Mr. Bumpy beside her, in the bed, no longer wetting it but still sucking his thumb, but happy with his presents piled on the night table and all down E's side of the bed (the baseball cap, the uniform, the model airplane and signed photograph of Lucky Lindy and the tomahawk and drum). You two should get some sleep, said Pauline, her dress rustling softly, her perfume acute in the stale-smelling flat. Yes, try to sleep, her husband said, and Bumpy can lie there beside you a while, and then they went out together for what E. called a night-cap and did not come back.

In years to come he blamed Pauline, but had been blame-less himself. In his version of their history he was set upon by his dear wife's dear friend, a harpy with bobbed hair. She wanted to destroy his marriage and his innocence; she had been envious, dissatisfied, and he had failed to notice this and perhaps had drunk a glass or two too much and so the two of them had ended up in bed. It had been, he claimed, an accident, a problem with the problems of the first trimester of a second pregnancy and the luxury of finding himself at one o'clock in the morning in his wife's rich friend's flat on the Isle St. Louis. It was the kimono, he claimed; he would blame the kimono and also the champagne. The best time, he wrote later, was the one that he and AnnaLise had had together in Paris, in the café or at the racetrack or in the Tuileries; the best time was when they were poor and happy and went skiing together before it all went bad.

Eve ate the apple first, E. wrote, and also drank applejack brandy and knew how to drape herself fetchingly with fig leaves, so in the interests of knowledge and a kind of full disclosure Adam urged her to take off her clothes. And therefore he had been not so much the seducer as seduced, although in the interests of full disclosure he had also been flattered, a little, and his judgment and sobriety were less than absolute. He would admit that much, he wrote, but surely if acknowledged a mistake could be forgiven. It was not my fault, it was never my fault, it was only the fault of the world. . . .

So her revenge will be to bring him the suitcase and to deliver it sweetly. Con not, that thou be not conned. Her revenge will be that E. will never know she's taken it, and his stories and his anecdotes will turn by turn appear. In, where is it, the *Frankfurter Zeitung* or *This Quarter* or *The Transatlantic Review*. In, where is it, *The English Review* or *Der Querschnitt* in Berlin or *Reader's Digest* or *Life* magazine. AnnaLise will destroy him with kindness and urge him to publish his work; she will place the bag upon the bed and say, Oh by the way I'm leaving you, these are the leavings and this is the last time we'll meet. You'll hear from my lawyers, I want a divorce, I don't have a heart left to break. It's over now, all over now, and I advise you to sign promptly and not to put up a fight.

E. would do so anyhow; he did not like to lose. He explained away the sheets by saying she should ask Frau Zimmer, who arrived every morning to start up the fire and haul away the coals. It must have been Frau Zimmer for he knew no one called Martha or Mary not to mention his wife's friend Pauline. Or at any rate not in that way.

The fire burns bravely, agreed AnnaLise, did you sleep with the landlady too? Have you no shame? Is there no limit to your self-regard and prevarication, you self-serving son of a *Hausfrau* from Winnetka? Did you have to seduce my best friend? In between the fourth and the fifth of what you call your stories I've inserted the relevant papers; please take and sign the documents in the indicated places and then we can without excessive fuss agree to our divorce. You publishing scoundrel, be damned.

So in this version of our history she does not lose the suitcase; she carries it to Switzerland and hands it to her husband and turns around and leaves. And he cannot bear to open it; he stows the words away. It is, for him, a talisman, a signal of the time his first marriage went bad and she left him with only language and went back to America and, in the due and proper course of things, began her life again. Years later AnnaLise forgives him; she marries an accountant and raises their two children and the children of her second husband's first marriage also; theirs is a large and happy family and they settle in White Plains. When—as happens still, from time to time—she thinks of E., his shadow no longer darkens the prospect or occupies her wakeful reverie or obstructs the view. She does not *forget* him precisely, because his photograph is often in the paper or magazines or on book jackets and in the windows of bookstores she passes; he has a certain public presence that she cannot avoid. But it is much more difficult to be the one who's left than to be the one who leaves and he cannot forget her easily. Too, he is a writer and retentive and the stuff of his life is the stuff of his prose.

The associations of the suitcase are painful, insupportable, and he hates it as he hates the fact she did not believe him or continue to believe in him and would not accept his explanation of Pauline. Oh, let it go. Leave it alone. In the pond of his life there will be other fish; in the book there will be other chapters, and plenty enough to go around. What we lose we can replace. He is a busy man, a celebrated author and full of ideas and commissions and projects to complete. Hawks, he avers, do not share. And although he cannot bring himself to abandon it entirely he has no need of the suitcase; it is abhorrent and implacable and reposes in his closet and moulders reproaching him there.

Thirteen ways of finding a suitcase:

1. In the closet, where you left it.
2. At your neighbor's, with whom you've been sleeping.
3. In the Dempster Dumpster, to which the remodeling crew consigned the contents of your study in error or perhaps at the not-entirely veiled suggestion or the active prompting of your soon-to-be-ex wife.
4. In the THRIFT SHOPPE, in the luggage section, surprisingly heavy and sold AS IS, so you must wait until you're home in order to jimmy the lock.
5. In a sale of personal effects, from the estate of the late Maud Morgan. Lot 49.
6. Because the airline has succeeded in recovery, its baggage service having traced it, having sent it first to Barcelona by mistake, then Tenerife, and finally returning the item five days later, with a knife mark on the surface they promise you can be repaired and for which they have made an allowance of $100, and if it cannot be repaired then the item is to be, or so they promise, replaced. You have been phoning them for days, and as often as three times a day. At last the good news comes from the customer service representative, who identifies herself as Henrietta with a deep-throated voice not unlike Lauren Bacall's, and when you tell her so she says, Yes, that's what my husband says. Who takes it nonetheless upon herself as though reading from a script (for, once we factor in the phrases that have

been used to placate customers from time out of mind, and factor in the limitations available to comfort when commercial, or the carefully couched explanation that will not admit to malfeasance or corporate responsibility or simply permit her to say, We're wrong, sir, we made a mistake, I'm sorry; I'm so sorry and we'll pay you whatever it costs— once we factor in such language it seems clear that Henrietta's spiel *is* script) to call you at home on Tuesday afternoon when otherwise you would be profiting from a not necessarily unaccompanied siesta, and who tells you that the item itself has been tracked to the airport in Athens. Well done, you say, well done, except I never even *went* to Athens and can't drink their retsina wine. But then the thing itself, *Das Ding an sich*, gets delivered at ten o'clock next morning by a driver with a moustache and a name tag saying Paddy and a cap set at a jaunty angle who accepts when you offer him coffee. He dawdles, it's his coffee break, and accepts a cookie also and discusses the vagaries of his profession and the hours he puts in on the road and the people he meets, some you wouldn't believe, in the middle of nowhere in the middle of the night. And so you oughtn't have worried, Ed, you didn't got to be nervous, and although he hasn't opened it it looks untampered with, except of course at Athens, but you know what they say about Greeks, the way they can't—here Paddy smiles, conspiratorial— keep their greasy little fingers to themselves. Just sign here, please, in triplicate, you get one copy I take two, yours is the yellow, mine the pink, the office keeps the white. This one has traveled more than most, this sucker kept us guessing, he admits, and Athens is a good place to avoid. Except for, what do they call the stuff, ouzo. And the traffic is the pits.

7. Having notified the bomb squad, since this object appears suspicious and you have no idea how it arrived at your office, officer, but have been receiving threats.

8. In the attic. The basement. The trunk of the car. Which, for reasons that escape you, the British call a boot.

9. At your publisher's, where in fact you've been rather too swozzled to remember you deposited it after that celebratory lunch at Le Pavillon, the one that your editor gave because of the bestseller list, the one you drove down for from Connecticut where you've been staying with Pauline, the one with soup and oysters and a rack of lamb and first a little drinky-poo and then chilled Piper Heidseck and then two bottles of Château Margaux and, with the sherbet, a sauterne just on the brink of turning but still splendid, splendid, and with the coffee Armagnac, and afterward cannot remember how you carried it into the office and said, Max, it's here, it's all in here, Max, it's my blood and guts and everything I know or ever *will* know how to write, my great bloody marked-for-death genius book.

10. Because a student sends a typed four-page double-spaced letter from the library in Middlebury, where the bulk of your papers reside and he's at work on his thesis and wondering if you might answer the following questions and be willing to provide, in the enclosed SASE, a summary of your intentions with reference to the suitcase in the Special Collection, his queries pertaining to how it arrived there uncollated and uncatalogued, and as an anonymous gift. He's been examining the suitcase in the Rare Books and Manuscripts Section, he writes, and wonders why you did not choose to publish the entries there contained. Too, he wonders if you'd

like a scribe, a *secretaire* around the house, he'll be graduated in the spring and his parents have promised him a graduation trip to France and Italy and, if he can afford it, Switzerland, but he resists the idea of graduate school and wants to be a writer too and understands the great tradition of apprenticeship and would be grateful for a reading list and would like nothing more than to answer your mail, which he knows you do not do yourself, he has heard of your famous refusals, but his aunt once knew you very well and told him when he inquired that perhaps her Schatzy wouldn't mind. Aunt Agnes sends her best, he writes, she's living in Key West.

11. Having advertised in *The Dial* and on the bulletin board at Shakespeare & Co. and *The Saturday Review*.
12. When you least expect it and where you least expect it, having abandoned the search.
13. For five dollars, and after repeated haggling, in the market in Kabul.

FOUR

I picture it this way:

She gets off the train.

AnnaLise is a writer, of course. She has been writing and reciting things as long as she or anyone who knows her can remember. She cannot remember a time, in truth, when she was *not* a writer—when words in their patterned arrangements were absent from her world. And she has been very well schooled. In even such a phrase as this—"when words in their patterned arrangements were absent from her world"—she notes the Anglo-Saxon influence in the opening alliterative emphases, the antecedent repetition of "remember" and that of the alphabet's twenty-third letter. Too, there is a hint—a first faint whiff—of epithet in the oral-formulaic "words in their patterned arrangements"; she copies the phrasing whole cloth.

As a child she made up patter songs until the cheerful nonsense with which she amused herself while burbling in her crib or pram appeared to make sonorous sense. *I'm a little teapot, short and stout,* for example, was a tune she liked to sing, or *You push the damper in, and you pull the damper out.* Note, please, the usage here of "crib or pram" —a contraction of the Latinate "perambulator"—suggesting to the attentive reader that our girl was raised in England or at least by Anglophiles, and that "pram" not "baby carriage" would have been her mother's—her nanny's?—habitual usage. And such words as "teapot" and "stout," as well perhaps as "damper," evoke the British Isles.

Where are we? I ask it again.

Before she could count she could spell. As a child she made up poetry for family occasions, in honor of her parents' birthdays or her uncle's wedding, and she fashioned long complicated rhymes in her head when playing with her rubber duck and goldfish in the bathtub or while she tried to fall asleep, insomniac at six. Is insomnia appropriate to a six-year-old, or should we rather think of her as language-haunted, unable to sleep? Note also, please, the transatlantic nature of such referents as "rubber duck and goldfish in the bathtub," suggesting in this instance not so much a place as a time. We do not antedate, apparently, the twentieth century's widespread deployment of yellow floating toys in bathtubs and its anxious post-Victorian insistence on immersion as a form of cleanliness. But are the goldfish plastic or real; is the anachrony here accidental or willed?

Our girl is a writer: repeat. Before she could spell she could sing. All her life she has been writing, and she has a gift for it, but it is not a gift she is ambitious to display. By the time A. entered college (Radcliffe College, A.B., Magna

Cum Laude, in the year of our Lord 19—) she had enjoyed a sufficiency not to say a surfeit of applause: the adults' smiling inattentive faces, the pat on her cheek or her knee. Perhaps her interest in the oral-formulaic tradition here also proves germane; she would rather speak her stories than endure their black reductiveness upon the flat white page. Her first printed effort—a villanelle on the subject of "Justice" in the high school literary magazine—has also been her last. She long ago renounced the idea of publication, which seems to her fruitless and vain. Like others of her class and sex she has no real concern for a career.

Instead she composes in secret and does not seek to show her work; simply to write it suffices. She has no interest in self-promotion or in being promoted by others; she does not enter contests or compete for literary prizes that may perhaps confer a fleeting fame. AnnaLise has a small inheritance and no present need to earn a living; she feels, indeed, a gentle scorn, if one may so express it, for merely commercial success. We are, let us remember, in an epoch long prior to this present age, when women felt no pressing need to be "professional." If some well-meaning someone approaches her—as happens still from time to time—with a request to read her writing she answers, always, No. It is, she says, a private occupation, like lying in bed with a book. One does it in silence, or should.

But it gives her pleasure to be otherwise with Edward and to let him know, from time to time, a little of that which she knows. She has taken him under her wing. His talent will require some severe self-tutoring if it is not to degenerate into mere fluency. And since her husband is not ready yet for accurate self-tutelage she acts as his tutor instead.

She offers him detailed critiques. She insists that he write every day. She corrects what he shows her each night. Three simple sentences in sequence that begin with the same three-letter pronoun and proceed to a present-tense two-syllable verb would not, for example, pass her hard muster or survive the original draft. But because of his masculine vanity, his *amour-propre* and prickly, not to say excessive, self-esteem, she teaches him in private and would deny in public what both of them know to be true: that credit, where given, belongs to them both. His achievement is, equally, hers. When his history comes to be written and the biographies accumulate, the critics will, to begin with, neglect or scant her role in his apprenticeship and argue that he taught himself, an autodidact from the first. It is not until the feminist and scholarly assessment, *Edward's Women: Between the Idea and Ideal*, written by Bernadette Auton and published by Virago Press in 19—, that AnnaLise receives her due. Now there are monographs about her, and early photographs have been unearthed, and from the people who made *Carrington* there's interest in a film.

For the three years since their marriage she has worked with him quite carefully, proposing that he read Balzac and Dostoevski and Flaubert. If she offers him a compliment, he's puppy-dog eager and proud. When his great friend Julian observed that the rich are different from you and me, Edward tried for a remark until he tailed off, sputtering, and ordered more chèvre and an additional bottle of wine. But she herself had answered, Yes, we have more patience in matters literary; we can afford to wait. Women are neither so involved in nor seduced by flattery as the pair of you appear to be; we may take its measure, *copains*. Note, please, the correct masculine usage of "chums" as opposed to, say, *copines*, which would render our present company without exception female. And is it mere folk etymology that argues a relationship between the two, as in the French word *pain* and the Latin *pane*? We break bread, do we not, in friendship and *cum pane*? And is this not what we choose to convey by the very word "company"—here she smiled at the waiter approaching their table with wine and cheese and the requisite basket of bread.

His apron was striped.

He smiled back.

And so when Edward's great friend Julian—so drunk she

wasn't even certain that he meant it or would remember next day—made a pass at her, he said he was attracted to her beautiful intelligence. That, and your bezoomies, he said. She told him, Nonsense, Julian, you need some sleep, and he said That's what I mean by your impeccable intelligence, you understand me, Lise.

Julian was famous already but Edward was not famous yet, and this caused a certain rivalry between them. The two men competed at tennis and shooting and in the important issue of who, without passing out, could drink a greater number of bottles of Sancerre. And then a restorative whiskey and then a restorative gin. They were like children together, always jockeying for position and soliciting her approval and hoping for applause. As though she might confer a ribbon on the victor in such contests, they did the standing broad jump and tap-danced for her benefit and in the men's room at Michaud's they discussed the question of virility. The two writers effected a comparison, while standing at the urinal, of penis size and manhood—which term itself is a form of synecdoche, as AnnaLise informed her husband afterward: the part representing the whole. According to Edward his own penis was the larger, but he did tend to exaggerate things and anyway, as she refrained from telling him, the size of a penis is not the only or even the principal thing that matters; there are other attributes—its extension, its rigidity, the duration of an erection—that matter as much if not more.

Thirteen ways of looking *for* a suitcase:

1. The next day.
2. The day after that.
3. Immediately. To the exclusion of all other matters and without consideration for or reference to the personal feelings of others, those friends and family members and business associates who seek to help or hinder, with an obsessive-seeming inattention to those who are searching for some *other*

suitcase, and with a total self-absorption and absolute consequent disregard for the way such a hunt might or might not affect them. Until I find it, fool. No I'm not thirsty, no I'm not tired, no I'm not hungry, no.

4. By advertisement. With a reward.

5. Systematically. Under the bed. In the closet. On the shelves at the end of the compartment, on the roof racks naturally, in the baggage cars ready for service or being cleaned at the Gare de Lyon and the porter's wheelbarrow and all along the platform and inside the station again.

6. Through hirelings. Wallace, I've misplaced my bag; would you contact the authorities and find it for me, please. Yes, Wallace, the leather one, the one with my initials, good, very good, thank you, many thanks.

7. Philosophically. What's gone is gone, done done.

8. Haphazardly. In fits and starts. Diligently then not so. For twenty minutes at a time, and then for ten, for five. *Morgenfrüh, domani, mañana en las tardes, le lendemain.*

9. In tag sales. In basements and attics. In pawn shops and antique shops and reconditioned leather shops. In clearance sales and yard sales and at auctions for impounded merchandise.

10. Wittily. Self-deprecatingly. As in the English actor's remark, when his career in the theater had faltered, that he would go to the left luggage office in Waterloo Station and say to the man at the desk, I have misplaced my talent. It's a little thing, a bright shining thing of no particular importance, but it does matter to me. I must have left it on stage by mistake, or been forgetful, or in a mad rush; if someone should return the thing, I'd be most grateful if you'd keep it. And I'll return tomorrow, I'll call back.

11. Witlessly. Self-aggrandizingly. You sonofabitch where's my suitcase? Where is it, you sonofabitch?
12. The twelve steps will fail to suffice. Nor can the stations of the cross, with their desolating pauses and the process unto Calvary, stand surety for or as an emblem of this pilgrimage. Whosoever seeks will not by definition find; who loses will not always gain.
13. Not at all.

For that was the beginning of the end. That was the spring when Paris was being discovered. Not by Parisians, of course, who had always known of its existence, and not by the English or Dutch or Italians, who knew about it also and looked at it askance. To those who could remember not only the Emperor Napoleon III but also his large predecessor the little Corsican; to those who can remember that *Paris vaut bien une messe* and cite not merely Henri de Navarre but Saint Louis and the period of famine when wolves ran freely through the district that we therefore call by its medieval sobriquet, the Louvre; to those who still hear tumbrils on the cobbled blood-sluiced paving stones the *vielle ville* is and will remain a city of dark light, of oxymoronic and Janus-faced corrupt intrigue and brutal treachery where their long-term enemies have for centuries conspired. This is the sort of sentence, reader, that for better or worse our heroine commends to our hero, and it suggests a near-total incompatibility of rhetorics; theirs was a clash of dictions from the start.

But none of this mattered that spring. What mattered were the crowds. The noise. The musicians and painters and dancers and poets and remittance men and, of both sexes, the drunks. Americans were busily discovering Paris, and came from everywhere enthusiastically, as though the River Seine and Notre Dame and the Eiffel Tower had never been in evidence before. They discovered the Left Bank and the Right Bank and were astonished to discover that there might be a difference between the two *rives* (could this be a folk etymology for "rivals," our AnnaLise would ask herself, or might a floodplain have been "riven" by the implacable Seine?), and vociferously the new *arrivals* stated their own geographical preferences and staked their several claims.

So it made good sense to leave. She and Ed had had enough of Paris that season; it was time to get away. He had been working on a collection of stories, and a house in the Alps, they agreed, would be productive and quiet and fine. He would find them a place among fir trees, a room they could afford with a view of the mountains, and as soon as he had finished skiing and found a suitable establishment and leased it for the springtime and perhaps the summer also she would come. He would miss her very much, he said, and she said of course she would miss him but the interval would make their reunion all the more exciting, would it not? In the interval she read Maupassant and visited the Louvre and wrote to her friends in America and also her family there.

(N.B. The usage of "pram" notwithstanding, we may now determine with some certainty that in this draft and chapter our lady is American. That nationality has already been suggested above by her having been matriculated at Radcliffe College of Cambridge, Massachusetts, but this fact alone need not have proved decisive, since those English girls who in that period eschewed or were not permitted the dubious pleasures of Oxbridge might well have attended Radcliffe instead. Nonetheless, the phrase "friends in America and also her family there" provides sufficient corroborative detail to settle the question at least provisionally and for our present purposes. She comes from Oak Park, Illinois.)

When the telephone rang that season it was always Julian, or so it seemed to AnnaLise. He was always asking if she cared to join him later for a concert or a party; he was witty and sad and urbane, and always he asked after Edward and whether they had found a chalet in the countryside and when she was planning to go. Not quite, she said, not yet. When Julian spoke about her husband it was in the terms of rivalry, and although he was the more successful at the present moment he seemed defeated already, as though he could predict the future and the future was not good. He was inconsolable, he said, at the prospect of her planned departure; she was the only one who understood him in this hour of most need. What are you talking about, she asked, and he asked, How can I be contented when my rival holds the field? It wasn't a fair fight, he said; he won your hand, o fair Yseult, before we even met. Before I laid my eyes on you, or anything else you'd permit: a finger, a garland perhaps?

He ran on and on in this fashion, comparing her to fair Yseult and Yseult of the White Hands; he could be amusing and sorrowful and glib. Your husband, Julian declared, is always ready and willing to help a person on the ladder of success. As long as that person—he stared at her unblinkingly—stands a rung or two above him on the ladder. Then we get a helping hand. Poor Julian had been so mournful on the topic of their rivalry that she was tempted to solace him and to provide the consolation he so vociferously desired and perhaps deserved. Too, she had been curious to find out about the size of his manhood and to discover if Edward had been telling the truth or if the terms—as she more than half suspected—had been in the telling reversed.

The terms had certainly been reversed with reference to writing size, for Julian's talent was large. He was a fine and accomplished writer, with three books to his credit, one of which was very good indeed, and his marriage was collapsing or perhaps had already collapsed. On the first Friday in May, accordingly, they went together to Chez les Vikings, and she listened to him describe his marriage and his difficulties with his wife, how she was having an affair with an airman and had been having the delusion that she was a ballerina, and then she spoke about her own marriage and her difficulties with Edward's prose. He'll learn, said Julian, he's getting better all the time and what you should do is teach him to use a red pencil and scissors, so he gets used to throwing things away, so he dispenses with his prose the way he does with friendship; why don't we go to bed.

They repaired to the Crillon—avoiding, as though by

unspoken agreement, their own nearby apartments and also avoiding the Ritz. In the Crillon, while she waited in the lobby, Julian engaged a suite, and both of them were nervous and embarrassed and uneasy, a little, because of their previous friendship and because of their discussion about the marital difficulties with her husband and his wife. It had been a mistake. They both had had too much to drink, and passed the point where alcohol excites expectation to the point where it reduces performance, and though she and Julian took off their clothes and he professed to admire the way that she looked and the beauty of her breasts and legs and her intelligence, in fact he fell asleep. Although she could find nothing wrong with the size of his synecdoche, its other attributes—rigidity, extension—did leave, at least in the course of that evening, in the large pink bed beneath the coverlet, a good deal to be desired. He had been saying something comical about champagne and, who was it? Ben Jonson, with his poet's impoverished insistence that his mistress Celia drink only with her eyes, because it saved a stirrup cup. Did AnnaLise know, Julian wanted to know, that tankards for women had pewter bottoms because you were supposed to raise your eyes above the rim of the cup in order to gaze at your partner? But tankards for men had glass bottoms instead, because you were supposed to see your adversary coming at you with a drawn dirk?

Drawn dirk, he repeated, drawn dirk, drawn dirk, drawn dirk, and then without any warning his face went deathly ashen and he commenced to snore.

AnnaLise lay rigid by his side. His breathing was not Edward's, not metronomic and comforting, and it took her a long time to fall asleep. Her dreams were populated by bullfighters and pregnant Indians and unimpressive middleweight boxers from Princeton, and had not been restful in the least. When she finally awoke next morning the two of them got dressed again and they discussed the situation and agreed that it was best this way; nothing had happened between them and there was no cause for regret. Her husband was in Switzerland, his wife was with her aviator, and that left the two of them upstairs at the Crillon.

They ordered orange juice and croissants and coffee from room service, and they sat at the table the waiter arranged and partook of their breakfast and talked. We could have been happy together, she said, and he said yes isn't it pretty to think so. In the terry cloth bathrobe the hotel provided, with his hair uncombed and not wearing glasses, the writer looked young and damned and beautiful, and she told him so and he said he was sorry, it just didn't work, I'm afraid, it isn't any good. Just take him his stories, said Julian, and make him burn his drafts.

Variations on the theme of "suitcase."

1. A briefcase.
2. A duffel bag. Louis Vuitton.
3. A steamer trunk, its corners reinforced, its strapping of a darker blue than is the trunk itself.
4. A knapsack. Eddie Bauer.
5. A garment bag.
6. A valise.
7. A *passepartout*.
8. A medicine chest.
9. A hatbox, golf bag, gun and rod case, picnic basket.
10. A gentleman's monogrammed calf-leather kit. Mark Cross.
11. A wooden crate.
12. A cardboard box.
13. The metal storage bin I bought once, after protracted haggling, for five dollars in the market in (cf. p. 132) Kabul.

So now on the train with her virtue intact she studies the suitcase her husband asked her to bring when he called. Coming back from the Crillon, she had let herself into the apartment and the telephone was ringing; she picked it up

and Edward said, Where have you been, I've been calling and
calling for hours. Because she did not like to lie to him or be
in an important way deceitful she said I couldn't sleep last
night, I went out comparative shopping and attended the
market, old shoe. I rang Julian also, he said, I thought perhaps he'd know where I might find you. Oh, said AnnaLise,
was he at home? and Edward answered No. She had known
this already, of course, but could not tell her husband that he
might find his rival in their suite in the Crillon. Instead for
Edward's benefit she described the flower sellers in the Place
de la Contrescarpe, the way the anemones looked, and the
dye that leaked beneath the trestle tables and a bedraggled
troupe of gypsies who were setting up a circus until he had
been mollified and said I must write it down sometime, and
she said, Yes, she couldn't write it herself, or not for publication, but of course her husband should. I've found a house,
he said, I've found the perfect place. Oh good, she said, oh
excellent. Would you bring along that suitcase, Daughter?
Edward asked her finally, and when she asked, What suitcase? he said The leather one in the hall closet, second shelf.

She booked a *couchette* the same night. The intactness of
her virtue had not seemed, in the morning, like cause for celebration; she was feeling a little bit sordid and more than a
little bereft. She rather liked poor Julian, with his extravagant talent and his rich awful lunatic wife. In spite of their
discomfiture, she had rather enjoyed the Crillon. So to distract herself as the train wound through tunnels and hillsides
dotted with steeples and sheep, after the border and the pleas-
antries with *Les Douanes* and because she sat in the carriage
alone (Where were the golden girls and lads; where was the
bustling conviviality of chimney-sweepers she had come, on
the basis of similar excursions, to take for granted on such
trains?) she retrieved her husband's suitcase (the gilt of the
lettering faded, the scratch marks on the metal by the keyhole, the torn and faded destination labels) and opened it up
and took out the stories he had asked for, the ones that she
hadn't yet seen. They had been neatly arranged, in file fold-

ers and chronological order; they were marked April 1, 2, 3, etc.; and his handwriting was good.

Now AnnaLise begins to read, believing that she might amuse or at least distract herself. This also will prove a mistake. This is far worse than the night before and the nothing that transpired in the hotel suite. She had hoped for consolation and instruction and distraction and to observe, from draft to draft, how very much Edward improved.

It is not as though she hoped to read Turgenev or Balzac.

It is not as though she expected something by Flaubert.

But these effusions of his are not stories, not even anecdotes or, what does he call them, vignettes.

But this language of his is atrocious, so very much a schoolboy's prose she cannot bring herself to think of it as Edward's work or the work of someone who could ever be a writer.

There are pages about football and baseball and boxing.

There are pages about fish.

That which she tried to teach him he has failed entirely to learn; that which he knows is not worth knowing, but bathetic and mannered and cheap.

His syntax is inventive to the point of incomprehensibility, and his lack of education is made manifest on every page; to say that she is disappointed is to say the least.

She is very glad for Julian's editorial advice, the day before, at breakfast, and very glad that, to her knowledge, Julian himself has never read her husband's schoolboy prose. For even in her shocked revulsion AnnaLise remains protective; she does not want the world to know how badly Edward writes.

There is a story about a canoe.

There is a story about weather and one about tying a fly.

But even to call them stories is to dignify them greatly and to pay them a compliment they don't deserve. They are, on average, two pages long. They possess neither structure nor point. They are mostly written out in pencil by someone with bad spelling and who uses words like this.

Once again we, reader, may observe the wearisome repetition, the triply deployed plural pronoun (*They, they, they*) with which these oversimple sentences begin and the paratactic avoidance of serial commas, not to mention, as it were, the apposite assertion and the dependent clause. *They* are, customarily, monosyllabic, and in those two words, "customarily," "monosyllabic," we have multiplied by more than five Edward's habitual not to say quotidian usage of language: what he likes are four-letter words.

She, AnnaLise, is appalled. His women are angels or whores. They marry for money or because they have money already; often they are lesbians and always their hair is cut short.

His men are not much better, though he knows rather more about men. His writers and athletes and soldiers betray in the manner of their drinking and the nature of their costume whether they are cowardly or brave. The subject of his stories in the deepest sense is landscape, but he piles the local color on in shovelfuls; he writes travelogues. He might have a future, perhaps, in the advertising profession or in Hollywood.

What to say?

Oh, what to do?

AnnaLise is feeling daunted but controls herself (collects herself?) and acts as though undaunted until she comes up with a plan. Between the villages of Pré-du-Lac and Interlaken she decides the best way to respond. On the off chance—a chance she doesn't dare to take—that Edward hopes to publish them, she will leave his stories on the train and declare they have been lost. Or stolen, impounded perhaps. I will leave the suitcase here not so much through inattention as intention, but if Edward asks about it then of course I must tell him the truth.

Deciding this, she smiles. She sees her reflection in the window of the tunnel and examines the cheekbones that Julian claimed so extravagantly to admire, the brown pageboy cut she acquired last week, and her teeth which, when in the American fashion she bares them by smiling, are straight and white and good. I will help my husband understand, she tells herself, the value of revision and the virtue of refusal and how we remember our successful lines in any case, rewriting, and how it is only a kindness to start out all over again.

There are things one does in one's childhood of which one is proud, naturally enough, and naturally enough also there are things one does in one's childhood of which one is ashamed. This is called a parallel construction with a hint of the chiasmus: Why I left your stories on the train was to improve them by absence and pack them, *Schatz*, as alms for oblivion; why I could not bring myself to bring them to you, Edward, is that you are better now, all better now, or so I fervently hope.

The porter appears. He knocks on her compartment door, announcing the second service in the dining car, and she rises, following, and takes a place at the last empty table by the window and orders a bottle of the chilled white Macon the waiter recommends. Or would Madame wish instead a bottle of Château d'Yquem? There are those who praise it highly, though I am not myself one of the admirers of Yquem, the waiter says, and unable to commend it to you without reservation.

The Macon, she says, as you suggest.

Very good, Madame.

And if they are acceptable an order of *bécaces*.

He extracts the cork with a flourish and then smilingly pours out a glass.

AnnaLise drinks.

It is best, she tells herself, not to admit to reading this; when he meets me at the station I shall say nothing at all. We will embrace and go to the chalet and resume, as it were, *la vie passionée* and I will answer his questions but ask him none of my own. My first opinion was correct three years ago when we first met and he said that he wanted to write, my reaction was accurate then. He should have been a

painter or a sculptor or even a collector; he must not continue to write.

But perhaps he will improve. No doubt he can improve. It
is, as Geneviève would say, incomprehensible, *affreux*; it is,
as Julian would say, unintelligent in the extreme. For it is an
atrocity to write so badly and so much, and a crime against
humanity to slaughter language so. Once more she lifts the
cold beaded glass from its place on the tablecloth up to her
lips. This too will pass, she tells herself, this too I'll forgive
and forget.

FIVE

I picture it this way:

She gets off the train.

Which, for years and years and pages and pages by now
has been her chosen mode of transportation.

Strange word, is it not?

With its suggestion of sensory transports, its secondary
meanings and elided implications, its evocative and half-
echoic consonance with that slant rhyme: transformation.

Strange world; is it hot?

She has been taking trains for what feels to us all like a
very long time, for decades, forever it seems.

AnnaLise has been consigned to trains for draft after draft
and in every kind of weather and nightly in my dreams.

As though probing the ambient air.

So it recurs, it is recurrent, it is a form no doubt of repetition compulsion: this near-imperceptible lift, this half-conscious preparatory shifting of the body's weight and its
potential energy now more precisely described as kinetic,
the right knee raised, the instep arched and toe outthrust
because our lady is right-handed and the right leg will be
therefore the one faring forward, o voyager, first.

And the platform, the platform, the platform, the platform.

Where I await her.

As usual. As always.

And the little newsboy says: If she stays, she stays, and that's all there is to it, he says.

While she gets off the train.

AnnaLise on the train.

Again and again and again and again and again.

So you found it? he asks.

I did.

When?

Next morning, she admits.

And where?

At the station, of course. Where we'd left it.

The station?

Indeed.

Forgive me, I thought . . . I was certain . . . I believed . . .

And were mistaken.

No.

You made a mistake, Edward, yes.

But was I not in my own mind and by some other someone's intention misled? By some god's intervention mayhap wittingly made witless?

Mistaken, I think. Just plain wrong.

It sat on the platform?

She nods.

It was waiting on the platform?

No. They called.

Who called? And who precisely, wife, is *they*?

The stationmaster. The conductor. I forget.

For*get*?

Let's not belabor this, *Schatz*.

All right.

Because we had no telephone, remember? Because you left the baker's number in case of an emergency.

If there was any news, he says, remembering, and then discerns her schoolmistresslike disapproval and corrects himself: If there *were* any news.

Correct.

It's the subjunctive. Yet more and more often in current usage . . .

Ignore current usage, my darling. Remember how we celebrated?

Yes.

How we both went back to collect it?

As soon as it stopped snowing. As soon as ever I could harness up.

Well, why did they take it?

He shrugs.

The *suitcase, Schatz.*

Now there you have me, Daughter. Wife. I just don't know. It happens.

And all the night before, she asks him, upstairs there, up in the chalet, did you think about the suitcase?

No.

While we were making love?

Of course not, no.

You can tell me.

A little.

And did it bother you? Were you concerned?

I didn't mind, not really.

Did it hamper your performance?

No.

Was I remorseful?

Yes.

Prettily?

Very prettily, yes. You are one of those women made lovely by tears. Others get all puffy-eyed and their skin mottles. Blotches. (Cf. p. 97.)

Oh, there were others?

No. Of course not.

And you made them cry also, I see.

Of course not, no.

Let's change the subject.

Yes. All right. He lights his pipe. Her cigarette.

Why did you wait?

Wait?

For all this time. So many years and pages. While all of us were worried sick. . . .

I didn't think you worried.

No?

I never imagined . . .

Then try.

And so in this draft, finally, the two of them are not in opposition. Instead, as they will later agree, they agreed. AnnaLise, arriving at the rented room, says Darling, there's something we need to discuss. And Edward responds, with his complaisant half-salute, that way he has of dipping his chin and smiling down at her, Fine.

The marriage will falter, admittedly, but in time to come and for different reasons. They will argue over Mr. Bumpy and his education and whether or not to return to the States and if E. should or should not continue as a journalist and whether F. Puss is a suitable watchdog and what kind of scooter to buy. When the doctors warn him that he must cut back on smoking and drinking or suffer the predictable damage AnnaLise will cease to smoke and drink and hope thereby to set a good example but succeed only in appearing—as he tells her when they argue—both sanctimonious and smug. Nor would the pair see eye to eye on voting rights for women or the nature of the reparations exacted by the Allies at Versailles; they will quarrel over Father Coughlin and how to deal with E's mother when she becomes incontinent and foul-mouthed and hair-tearingly insane. They will disagree on many things but not about the suitcase; this is a shared decision and marital accord. It is the topic of that week in Schrunz, the issue they try to resolve.

And the decision will be reached not in anger but loving-kindness; it is a story they make up in bed. And, later, over coffee and still later over kirsch. While Frau Zimmer stokes the wood stove and the snow falls thickly, silently, drifting past the windows, and in those intervals each afternoon when it does not snow and the sky turns bright blue, they are happy with the sausages and cheese and *glühwein* in double-handled glasses, and they are very much absorbed by the problem of the suitcase she has carried with her carefully and brought to the chalet undamaged and they discuss the problem in terms of both manner and matter, *forme et fond*, while Bumpy is learning to ski. He toddles off with the instructor—waving at the two of them, wearing mittens and the blue and yellow scarf she crocheted last summer, his nose already bright and red, his eyes that astonishing still-baby blue—and mother and father can talk.

What AnnaLise says to her husband is this: I love you, I adore you as a writer. I think you're wonderful and believe in you absolutely. But these stories are our secret and you spoil it by writing them down. Oh, darling, don't be angry, I can't bear it when you frown that way, they are excellent stories, I promise, they are absolutely wonderful, but once you publish them you'll make it so our secret isn't private any more and they'll copy them and sell them much too cheaply and I'm already feeling rotten to be so, oh, what's the best way to express it, *available* to strangers and their prying eyes. Because you write about our time together in Paris and I don't want the world to share it, it will be our little secret like the way you call me *Schatz*. I don't want the world to read and spoil it, all that part about the train. Or the part about Pauline. We won't discuss it, Tatie, we won't disagree or wreck it but I want to say this brightly and tell you to look at it later, much later, when we have gained perspective, declares AnnaLise; when we're not so much in the middle of things and this is ancient history, not very recent fact.

All right, he says, all right. It's only because I believe in you so, she repeats. And afterward she says Let's all go skiing together, let's wake Bumpy from his nap and pack a lunch and then tie on the sealskins and walk up the side of that mountain again and schuss down on new snow.

But I describe it more briefly than it in fact transpired; E. does not agree at first or concur without regret. A. needs all her delicacy and her skill at handling him and even, let us admit it, her guile. He resists her, to begin with, saying that she understands some things about life and he understands other things about art, and what she fails to understand is that these stories are a testimony to their shared youth and happiness and that at least two members of what the *garagiste* considers a lost generation have not been lost but found. They may be childish things, he says, but they're *my* childish things. She says, Well, of course if you decide to they're your stories and your property but as far as I'm concerned it's a mistake. As far as I'm concerned it's something you should put aside and be grateful and proud to have written but not make a public display. Then she strokes his neck and strokes his back and does the thing with both her hands between his thighs that he particularly likes and says, See, some pleasure isn't public, some delight is not display.

On the third day he yields.

So together they concoct a story for the press. Well, not at this stage for the press, since there are scarcely any journalists in Wengen, or was it Zaas-Fe. Those who compose their stories for the *Allgemeiner Tagesblad* or the *Zurischer Zeitung* (cf. p. 74) are not inclined to write a column about luggage and as-yet-unimportant writers and uneventful journeys taken on a train.

But later the tale will prove useful; later it will help to have an explanation of what happened or what failed to happen and why these anecdotes and recollections and, yes, let us call them stories did not see the light of day. Edward and AnnaLise announce that she arrived without his suitcase, with the drafts and pages stolen or at the least misplaced.

But this is not what happened, not at all.

What happened is she said to him, I've brought your stories, darling, just the way you asked me to. Everything is here and all of it intact. But you could do me a great favor and refrain from publication; you could wait. In, who knows, twenty-five or thirty years you can use them again; I'll be old; I'll be elsewhere or forgetful or maybe even dead. For art is long and life is brief and when he asks who said that she says, I think, Hippocrates, and he says In my short life I've not seen an arse more perfectly proportioned than yours and she says Don't distract me old shoe and don't let's joke about it because I'm being serious. If in twenty years or so you see fit to use these stories then by all means do so, and do so with my blessing. Only not now please not now.

And he, who is impatient, learns patience from her and, in a gesture of submission, says yes all right for your sake OK. They agree that his genius stories were lost in the Gare de Lyon. They agree that it has been her fault and that he does not blame her but has hurried back to Paris to make sure. For the rest of the week they refine their alibi on the mountain and in the Konditorei while Bumpy eats his chocolate cake and, later, in the bed. She does the Edward imitation and he the AnnaLise; they change places the way he likes and when she's finished with the scarves and leather ankle straps and Frau Zimmer asks permission once more to change the sheets and light the stove they have attained a satisfaction and exhaustion both at once. For he knows she has done him a favor and after some time he admits it and, although it is his habit to blame others and absolve himself, he behaves rather better than usual and admits that her judgment's correct.

When his editor asks, he says Lost. When Scott and Sherwood and Gertie and Alice and Fordie and the rest inquire he says, Gone. When in time to come it proves to be a commercial matter of some consequence he says, Stolen. Who knows how? He says that he returned to Paris and went to the flat, not believing the loss could be total but found nothing there at all. Well, one story about Liz and splinters on a dock. And one about fathers and sons. But the cupboard was bare and poor doggie had none and he repressed the memory and could not bear to look for it and could not bear to think about it until much later on. And when much later the reporters and biographers and critics press him on this matter he makes a little mystery, saying We know when and where, not how; we know only two thirds of the mystery story, only that she came to see me and was carrying the suitcase and it was lost in the Gare de Lyon. And AnnaLise herself will say, Oh, whatever was I thinking when I left it with the porter, I got off the train and wept and wept, oh all my life I'll rue this day and why did we ever flee south?

There are refugees from Schicklgruber and Mussolini and Franco who will flee south in bitter truth; there are those who must carry their most precious objects, their documents and silver, in the one car that runs out of petrol or the cart that gets mired in mud. Others faint on the road and fall starving or dying or get shot as malcontents or traitors or spies or malingerers; there will be mass displacement and horror and despair. There are those who carry on their backs or in their arms their heirlooms and children and family albums, and there are many tragedies more actual than imagined and much that is much more important gets lost. There are many more serious stories, reader, as all of us agree.

But this story of theirs is remembered; this object feels totemic and when he turns to it, as AnnaLise predicted, not after her death but the death of their marriage, not in twenty or in thirty years but forty years thereafter, when he opens it once more the wind that coursed through the cedars down the mountain and then through the bedroom in Schrunz comes gusting out replete with that most private grief, the past.

For the years and the gin take their toll. Time marches on, then limps. What follows are his notes. What he composes decomposes; what he writes he rewrites and rewrites. He loses his memory, loses his hair. He repeats himself often and badly. What follows are his notes.

The Closerie des Lilas.

Evan Shipman.

Ezra.

Then T. S. Eliot maybe, and maybe Jimmy Joyce.

Ernest Walsh. Robert McAlmon.

And then the damned poet, the *poète maudit*, the young man marked for death.

Lyon.

How thin we were how hungry and how ambitious how poor.

Except for the trust fund, of course.

And, later on, the motorcar.

How happy then beneath the sheets, and never cold together.

With a headwaiter who remembers you and a thermometer under the armpit and grease.

The Select.

The Dôme.

The Deux Magots.

When our Edward finds he cannot work he opens the suitcase again. The key will not turn in the lock. He forces it; it breaks.

The ink on the foolscap has faded, the typescripts show their carbons and seem a kind of cuneiform carved on clay tablet or reed-brushed characters on joined papyrus: ancient implements deployed in ancient days. A crumbling leather backing and a criss-crossed knife slash (made in Athens? Barcelona? Tenerife?) visible athwart the suitcase top. A label that peels at the touch.

Yet here, inside, astonishingly, his language lies before him.

Sheet on sheet in ordered sequence and only a little bit brittle with age, only a little bit dog-eared and brown.

An odor of dust; dry stale air.

The pages that he put away against this rainy day.

As she had suggested he should. Predicted he would.

At first he cannot quite believe it, parsing the phrases rapidly, then more carefully through paragraphs, then word by word through stories, the record of their time together, all those tales he thought he'd jettisoned about the way it was and could not ever be again because it has been spoiled by time and chance.

But here, as in a fairy tale, restored.

And perhaps a certain shame attaches to the notion that losers are weepers and finders are keepers, particularly if and when the finder is also the loser, the two men are one and the same.

In their agony of repetition, in their history retrieved.

For it is not always or only the case that what is lost stays lost.

So this was the speech I gave, getting that prize, this was the way that it went. Ladies and gentlemen, friends, honored judges and beloved colleagues and students amongst whom there is one who will someday assume the podium where in white tie and tails I now stand. My heartfelt thanks, my deepest gratitude. In this community of shared endeavor, this guild wherein apprentice and journeyman—or should I rather say journey*person*—laborer are one, let the torch be passed, the word go forth, the row on row of poppies blow until the crack of doom. Let it be understood by each and all that we are not so much the messengers as message and the thing relayed, the written or pronounced occasion that permits a time and place to grow articulate until the last drawn breath tamps down, until there be a gargling or a glottal stop. Rising up through the distillate silt of the well, rising high in the throat of this old man of sorrows who ain't quite finished yet.

Who still has a story to tell.

Who has ransacked his history and opened the locked suitcase and found those sketches long forgotten and never in any case sufficiently well rendered that describe the flower sellers in the Place de la Contrescarpe.

The gypsy girl in Cavaillon, or was it Aix-en-Provence?

The bald little genius Spaniard, or was it Mr. Cezanne?

The Seney stretch, the hotel where they billeted fathers and sons. The three-day-blowing western wind and small rain raining down.

Until everything was wreckage while they ogled you, the journalist and the *notaire,* the butcher and baker and my great friend the phrasemaker Julian.

The skiing trip in Manitou where we lashed the frozen bear on skis and made a sled of it and brought the carcass to town.

The recipe for *soubise à l'ail* that Jean-Jacques or let us call him Anders acquired while appticed in his uncle's tavern in the hills above Lausanne.

And also the *berühmte croque-monsieur.*

Who has kept this cache a secret until now. Who did not seek to publish it before. Who discovered carbons that she left, and in the rear left corner of the second shelf of the hall closet in the Paris flat what until this very paragraph he'd thought he lost, although he could remember taking it with the negligent peremptory attentiveness of youth from the outstretched right hand of the woman he loved. Which hand he could imagine and would soon enough render actual above his shirt, then descending as she liked to do not as when one throws a stone into a pool's unblemished surface and may see the ripples widening, the circumference enlarging, but rather in a series of ever more constricted circles, the interlocking cones of memory, so that her first such gesture may incorporate both toe and throat, the next both knee and chest, the last both rib and clavicle. You get the picture, reader, you understand why he anticipated, as did once the raider of cities or red-haired Menelaos, that warm immersion in the bath, that upraised finger, downturned palm, that hand he took as tentative of what would follow as the night the day once he could get her to the rented room, and the by-no-means-negligent and all-encompassing desire for word made flesh and flesh made wordless. So that when at last she comes to him, stepping as though laved by oil from the hot cauldron of the train, stepping down the metal rungs and passing the conductor, then handing him her bags or dropping them beside his feet and skipping as though for all the world unencumbered into the circle of his open arms, while they perform this oh-so-cruelly delayed and ah-so-long awaited and accomplished *pas de deux*, the leg on leg, the lip on lip, Oh darling, she says, how I've missed you, did you miss me? *Did I, Do you like my beard, Yes, oh yes, And should I shave it, No, oh no*, and how for five whole weeks I've waited for this day. And then inside his rented car on the atrocious goat track that they call in this *verdammte* country a road, and then the chalet he's so proud to have found, so pleased to have leased for two dollars a day, does it meet her approval and does it matter? Will she tell the truth? As though already stepping lightly from the shower she requires after travel and before their first sustained embrace, *because I want to wash it off, wash it away*—the stink of strangers, stench of otherness, the grime of the train's headrest—*and make myself pure for you, dear. Ten minutes more and it will have been worth it, I promise, I'll make myself ready, wait here till I call you*, and then taking the soap, accepting the towel the landlady provides and gazing at him over her shoulder with that blithe unspoken invitation and stepping for the moment softly out of his line of sight and away from his devouring gaze: with all of this and more in the forefront of his consciousness and the preparatory tingle of tumescence and the pricking of his upraised thumbs, the last thing Edward cares for is some stories in a suitcase, the least of his concerns is a valise.

But what of the living, the dead; what of the quick and the calm? *What happened to you afterward, my darling, how could you continue without me?* What, when you speak of this years from now, will you yourself say and who blame? *What will we say of them, write of them, sing of them; what can be reconstructed when they both forget?* Is all this important to her also or a half-forgotten episode? In the skein of her life when she weaves and describes it how colorful will be this strand? *What is it, I wonder, about the apparatus of celebrity, the lobster on the leash or habit of cigars or love of bullfighting or espousal of fascism that remains remembered when the language as such has been lost?*

The suitcase the suitcase the suitcase the suitcase: How could you have left it there, why?

There have been other versions. There was the AnnaLise grown old or, if not old, corrupt and practiced; there was the AnnaLise who understood, as I do not, the sonorities of the Swiss horn; there was the film star, the writer, the critic. Still others wait in the wings.

For she will leave him, she has left.

And he will leave her too.

Retaining only the books on the shelf, the placards and awards on walls, the shelves in the library bulging.

The letters he writes her, the letters she wrote.

The phrases and the sentences and paragraphs and chapters.

The stories and the novels and, what does he call them, vignettes.

Poor Julian, poor Madame LaBecque and Geneviève and Anders M. Hoffman's idiot child and his devout cowering wife.

Poor all of us, all of us, all.

Yet when she exits finally, might she nonetheless return; does she come back to take a curtain call; can their affair resume? Is this a fleeting dalliance or a permanent enthusiasm?

A commitment, as it were.

Exit the writer and his lady. *Exeunt omnes.* Pursued by a bear.

As Petrarch to Laura so Dante to Beatrice or Keats to Fanny Brawne; as William Shakespeare of Stratford to the conjectural dark lady of the sonnets, so Flaubert to Louise Colet.

But these are large examples and talents exemplary, reader; we speak here of less.

But in the case of Edward? AnnaLise?

It is over, *es ist vollbracht.*

Because of course she cannot stay, not even in his memory, unaltered or without reference to fashion. Things change, it is in their nature to change. Our idea of beauty will alter, as must by definition our inspiriting ideal. Consider the Hottentot Venus, then Nefertiti, then Saskia and the Maija Desnujada and this season's supermodel and next season's candidate, and then contrast and compare.

For what is a suitcase, what sort of a gift? What has she left him with, leaving him that? The memory, perhaps, of what he once produced; the receptacle of all his early effusiveness—the proof in dog-eared black and white that once he was a young man and an enthusiastic and energetic beginner poised above his work desk, rapt. Who had believed the suitcase stolen, the language in it long since lost, but he has always been a lucky man and she a large part of his luck. Imagine for a moment, reader, that you too are young again, the world before you like a path of gold, the first kiss or million dollars or the perfect game awaiting your first toss toward home plate. Imagine that it's Eden still, this overgrown garden we have decided not to prune or weed or hoe. With wandering footsteps and slow. Or that the night is sleepless since you do not *choose* to sleep and that you could at will and readily drift off. What was possible remains a plausibility and what was lost is found. Imagine that your AnnaLise returns in all her original beauty, her unblemished innocence, and that age has neither withered nor custom staled her infinite consistency, that she is the dream you first dreamed. These paragraphs are yours, were mine; they have been waiting in this suitcase for longer than we care to count, and now have been by your conceiving—great word of art and life—restored.

I picture it this way:

    She gets off the train.

    AnnaLise gets off the train.

One final time our girl gazes about and construes her own shadow and stares down the length of the snow-sprinkled platform. At mountains, a porter, a conductor, a dog.

She represents, of course, the Muse; in whatever way such visitations happen and for whatever reason (his quick grin, his insouciance, his nine-inch cock?) she finds herself compelled by Edward. She has watched him for some time, watched *over* him for years. Perhaps already in his crib, perhaps in grade school or junior high or during the period of his apprenticeship to the school yearbook and the newspaper, more probably one morning in the bathtub at the age of six when he found himself, with no discernible prompting, able to remember whatever he had heard that day or read the night before and able to rhyme and recite it—when he woke, I say, to the glad awareness of language, this repeated glad awareness in and of itself appeared involuntary and not in the strict sense rational, as though he were a tuning fork and some composer struck a note, as though he were the subject of this sentence and not object or as though the two were—awful word—conflated or—slightly less awful—linked.

But whatever the reason, having elected him as vessel, AnnaLise has poured herself unstintingly within.

And although our hero is an egotist, he is neither wholly unaware of nor ungrateful for the honor. In the watches of the night or bent above his writing desk he does feel singled out. He thinks of writing as a trade, a craft, a discipline, and has apprenticed himself to it gladly; his pleasure in the work of words is real. He suspects himself to be Muse-blessed and understands that he is fortunate but perhaps not quite deserving. From time to time when drinking gin or in the fleeting interval between night wakefulness and sleep Edward hears, or tells himself he does, the beating of great feathered wings.

Above, about him raised.

Upon the ambient air.

For, for all her corporeal splendor, what she is is his *idea*.

And so when AnnaLise descends the staircase of the train she moves toward him floatingly, a disembodied image of a naked lady, hovering; as though what they have done together is mere prelude to a chess game or act of intellection, as though each of their shared intimate endeavors must be both *in* the field and *of* it, both the prospect and the retrospect of luck.

And he her willing servant and her self-appointed slave.

The strap of her sandal, the comb in her hair.

The parabola that she inscribes while stepping, the sine curve of her outstretched arm and therefore upraised breast.

For, from the long-established vantage of her Olympian distance, she has surveyed the field. She plays it only selectively, sitting on the shoulders of few each generation. She invades even fewer: five, six.

They have been recently married; their marriage will not last.

Is it she who will leave him, her fancy alighting elsewhere, her attention for a moment or eternity distracted?

Or, less plausibly, he her?

And if this is so, in what way?

In the various infidelities, the need for admiration, the lust for reporters and contracts. Inattention, exhaustion perhaps. The preference for—oh, skeet shooting, trout fishing, automatic writing, rum. The self-delighting self-affrighting pleasures of music, the tune in his head, *da dum, dum diddy dum*. The customary deployment of room service, Marlene Dietrich, oysters Rockefeller, Cindy Crawford, and Château Petrus. The habitual availability of—oh, bullfights and football and off-the-shoulder velvet evening gowns and cummerbunds and cocaine. Death in the afternoon, *la mordida*, sauce béarnaise, Strauss's *Allerseelen* in the gathering deep dark. The various antidotes of conversation and in nature, the grim distraction of the news, the seductions of torpor and a TV interview at midnight and that last refuge of the scoundrel: politics.

Madness.

Lewdness.

Cowardice.

Loss.

And therefore bit by bit and almost imperceptibly over time our hero—once so severe, so constant of purpose and disciplined in habit—permits himself to take her not so much for granted as for something of less value than it was to start with: a currency debased. Soon what has begun as attitude becomes a routine condescension, a familiarity that serves him as first cousin to contempt. A diminution of his capacity for wonder, a sense there's nothing singular in being singled out like this and that she is but footnote to his text.

Till one fine morning he wakes up and, as always, stretches and, as always, shifts the pillow and thrusts back the blanket and gets out of bed, gingerly testing his right leg, his hip, the stiffness in his joints, the muscles of his back, his throat engorged, his mouth still tasting like the bottom of a birdcage, and shuffles to the bathroom where he runs the tap and spits and rinses off his teeth, blinking, pissing, hawking phlegm, and turns on the overhead light and switches on his own electric kettle for the first cup of hot water with lemon, since he does not want to bother the night nurse or, more precisely, to be bothered by her, cannot *bear* to share the fuss and ruckus of conversation at this hour but instead surveys the landscape (sea grape, sea fog, the rising sun and fading moon and could that be the Southern Cross?) and throws back the green wooden shutter and latches it, as always, to the black hook in the stuccoed wall and sits to his work desk, as always, positioning the cane-backed chair, sharpening his pencils and smoothing out the foolscap and reading what he wrote before, the verbiage accumulated yesterday and also the day before that, sucking maybe on a gumball, staring at the palm tree and the cactus back beyond the pool, sitting poised as though expectant of, attendant on *her* visit, her seductive tactile presence on the naked yellow unlined sheet, for he has worked this way for months, for years, for decades, every morning in this fashion at this hour and no matter what has gone before, how hard the night or troubled the sleep, how many words he wasted on and with how many incidental players, undone, unstrung, half comatose, so that it is merely accurate and neither boastful nor self-serving to report the yield was real, the harvest abundant, the language *available* to Edward—witness the books on the shelf, the placards and awards on walls, the shelves in the library bulging—and so it takes him longer than it should have, possibly, to sense how something else obtains this day, some alien vacuity enters the room, or how the light comes slanting in without illumination.

The palm trees do not frame his view, and what he has for company is absence and not presence.

Not AnnaLise.

The habit broken, the pattern no longer ingrained.

The song he taught himself to hear is silence now, not with him now, not this fine morning at his desk and, although he does not wish to admit or consciously consider this he knows it already, irrevocably, once gone it is gone and will not return to him ever, nor come to him again.

As once in May.

Letter to a Young Fiction Writer

February 17, 1999
Ann Arbor, Michigan

Dear Franz K:
You don't exist. Well, all right, you did exist, but your last name's not Kafka and very few remember you except as a recipient or, as your teacher might have said, a *receptacle*, a *vessel*. Rainer Maria Rilke wrote letters to you long ago, and they are what we have. You are and were the young poet—strange convention of critical discourse, that we employ the present tense—to whom he dispensed and dispenses advice. "The blue-sealed letter bore the postmark of Paris, weighed heavy in the hand, and showed on the envelope the same beautiful, clear, sure characters in which the text was set

down from the first line to the last." That's what you wrote, remembering, from *Berlin, June, 1929.*

That the letters should remain in print is no small credit to your powers of attention and retention; you do survive as witness and conservator, Herr K., and for this you have our thanks. Thanks also for the modesty with which you excised your own missives to him, the ones that he so scrupulously answered but that have been long since lost. *Letters to a Young Poet* fails to amount to a shared correspondence, replicating turn by turn the letters *from. . . .*

Or perhaps you kept no copies of the lines you wrote, and probably he didn't bother to preserve them; you were neither rich, nor female, nor famous. Too, he traveled a good deal those years, and no doubt he thought—who can blame him?—that he'd discharged his debt to you by writing and tore your letters in two. Then the great man let your stationery flutter to the floor for servants to collect, or balled the fragments up and tossed them into the fireplace negligently, or left them behind in the hotel or guest room escritoire when he traveled on. At any rate, my friend, the conversation was one-sided—an interrupted monologue—and you'll forgive me if I follow where he led. He *used* you, Franz; he was ready to answer your questions and you furnished the occasion and after he expressed himself he dropped off your personal map.

So too will I. These lines are a "one-off," a variation on a theme, and I want to use you—to quote another poet of a slightly later era—in order to mix those paired ingredients, "memory and desire." I've been teaching now for a very long time, have produced unnumbered thousands of pages in response to student writing, and since I remember what it meant to read such letters early on I take this chance as a high charge: I want to tell you what I can about the world of words.

And yet the topic daunts. Not so much the topic, perhaps, as our collective title—with its tipped cap to Rainer Maria Rilke and the otherwise-forgotten Franz Xaver Kappus. You who sat on a park bench in 1902, with a book by Rilke on your lap, and were moved to write him and engender a response. Like that person from Porlock who interrupted Coleridge in the dear dream of "Kubla Kahn," Herr Kappus deserves a footnote in literary history; without you we'd not have this record of advice. You both went to school at the Military Academy in Wiener-Neustadt, and neither of you liked the military life; your letter touched a nerve. Not all that hard to do with Rilke, let's admit; he was neurasthenic to a fault, and ready as a tuning fork to vibrate when properly struck.

But the "young poet" must have been astonished; he sent off some apprentice verse and reaped a returning whirlwind from Paris, then Viareggio, then Worpswede, Sweden, and Rome. There are ten of these epistles; they span the years from 1903 to 1908. The first of them is dated four years short of a century ago: *Paris, February 17th, 1903*. Sometimes hectoring, often runic, always generous, the pages set a standard it's not easy now to meet: Rilke wrote with a sense of his own consideration and a high grave consequence, one eye fixed upon eternity and one eye on the clock. . . .

So yes, my dear Kappus, I swallowed you whole. I was trying to learn German, and the M.D. Herter Norton translation served admirably as trot. The letters gave an early clue as to what it might entail to make of writing a profession. I had been given a copy of *Briefe an einen jungen Dichter* by an uncle who well understood I hoped to be a writer; he himself had translated Rilke from his own *Muttersprache* in order to improve his sense of the English language and the diction to which, courtesy of Adolph Hitler, he had been as an adult consigned. My uncle knew great swatches of the Duino Elegies by heart, and he would nod approvingly while I recited too. Once when I offered up, from Rilke's *Notebooks of Malte Laurids Brigge*, the defining phrase: "*Er war ein Dichter, das heisst, er hasste das Ungefähr*," my uncle asked, "But how would you translate it?"

" 'He was a poet,' " I ventured. " 'Which is to say, he despised the approximate.' Or perhaps, 'hated the inexact.' "

"Not bad," he said. "Not bad. . . ."

I was a senior in college. My thesis dealt in part with Rilke's *Neue Gedichte*, and everything about the man compelled me: his intricate affairs, his picturesque quasi-poverty, his time with the sculptor Auguste Rodin, his passive-aggressive hovering near aristocrats, preferably female, his prose, his listless energetic pose, his verse. How splendid it would be, I thought, to wander the world making sonnets and sit in lamplit circles sipping wine from crystal goblets while, somewhere, a lutenist strummed. I dreamed of full-skirted consorts on the beach near Bremen and read the biography of Lou Andreas-Salome with near-prurient delight. Oh, Rilke was my Yeats. The castle walls, the words from the wind, the stagey stages of a career and death of a rare blood disease—pricked by a rosebush, he failed to recover—all these were just the thing. *Das ding an sich*, the thing itself, the *thingsomeness*, the *thingliness*, would furnish my aesthetic as it had structured his. Even his early and pretentious rhyme (who really reads the *Erste* and *Frühe Gedichte*?) then struck me as good news, a sign that one could get better by *willing* it, and a sense of vocation sufficed.

By now I'm not so sure. The poet's eyes that seemed so luminous with pain and bliss in the old photographs strike me, today, as watery, and the moustache droops. Rilke was only twenty-seven when he began to write to Kappus, and much of the elder young poet's advice looks merely inward-facing: Narcissus in the mirror if not pool. The roses and the maidens and the lighthouses and the Orphic utterances— "The love which consists in this: that two solitudes protect and limit and greet each other"—now seem a little humid to me, and poor long-suffering Clara Rilke put up with a good deal. The characteristic *Leben sie wohl!*—the "Live well" with which RMR concludes a letter—is often as not self-serving or at least self-dramatizing; why bother to harangue poor Kappus, insisting that, like some sort of cobbler, he needed to stick to his last?

Whatever the motive, and whether causal or coincidental, the effect of Rilke's hortatory instruction was that his pupil ceased to write: "life drove me off," Kappus later admitted, "into those very regions from which the poet's warm, tender and touching concern had sought to keep me." Well, perhaps . . .

But it's unkind to satirize the sacred texts of one's own youth or to reclassify those sacred cows as bull. Like *The Prophet* or *Siddhartha, Letters to a Young Poet* is a young person's book. I can't read it now with the wide-eyed wonder that obtained when I first found the volume; there's too much heavy oracular breathing and faith in the privileged self. Too small a proportion of the ten letters deals with the work at hand, too much with the as-yet-unwritten ideal; my own best notion of how to help students has more to do with close reading and "the thing itself."

Still, these are talismanic texts: Franz Kappus tapped a golden vein and Rilke's mine was rich. And the great line at the end of the great poem about the archaic torso of Apollo rings true to me today—truer, perhaps, than at first encounter. It remains a clarion call to the young fiction writer as well as to the poet: *Du musst dein Leben ändern.* "You must change your life."

This season I've learned two new lessons about what might as well be called the literary life. My own has had a disconcerting longevity by now; though I think of myself as a schoolboy with his satchel and shining morning face, I'm someone who published his first novel more than thirty years ago and should probably wear trifocals. It's been a longish haul. So it's perhaps not surprising that the landscape alters or that there be milestones in a marathon—but these two do look like markers to describe.

The first is wholly happy and a cause for celebration. In 1984 I was teaching in a workshop, the Breadloaf Writers'

Conference in Middlebury, Vermont. This is a place where tuition-paying amateurs show their work to putative professionals in the hope of affirmation; in theatrical terms it's the equivalent of an open casting call. Each of the staff members was assigned some twenty or so such hopefuls; they'd been told to provide us with manuscripts and then foregather in class.

One of the works, I remember, was a pearl among white peas. The story was called "The Apple Picker Hits the Road," and it seemed letter-perfect to me then, and it does so still. Its author turned out to be a silent, lanky, nervous young woman in the corner of the room; she had not shown her work or received encouragement before. I next asked to see the novel she confessed to have been working on for years. It was full of amateur errors, and I said so, and that seemed to establish some trust between us; she'd been wary of what she took to be unfounded praise but responded with real interest to a sustained critique.

So we remained in touch; we wrote letters and saw each other intermittently; when the time came I invited her to give readings here in Ann Arbor and teach in the graduate writing program for which I served as director; over the last ten years or so I've watched her shelf of books increase with something very like paternal pride. Her name is Andrea Barrett; one of her recent efforts, a splendid collection of interlocked tales called *Ship Fever & Other Stories*, received the National Book Award for fiction in 1996. To return to my opening trope, if a career may be described as a race, I've had the chance to watch Ms. Barrett start in a crouch and hit her stride and break the tape; she has, as it were, breathtakingly arrived.

The second milestone is less pleasant to describe. More than twenty years ago (the summer of 1977) my late colleague at Bennington College, John Gardner, and I began a Summer Writing Workshop in a kind of conceptual opposition to the model of Breadloaf itself. Instead of students bringing what they thought of as accomplished prose for a thumbs-up or -down, we planned to accept only those who wished to labor at their projects while enrolled. Revision was expected and new drafts encouraged; our sessions resembled not so much an audition as rehearsal, and we read—or so it seems to me in retrospect—a prodigious amount of language from young and middle-aged and elderly writers who emerged from year-long solitude to share what they'd produced. . . .

We kept them in town for four weeks while great practitioners like John Cheever and Bernard Malamud dropped by to monitor progress; it was a heady time. The next year we repeated and expanded the venture, adding other genres (poetry, nonfiction) and offering a two-week option for those who could not stay the month. The notion took root and flowered and by now has flourished mightily; it's difficult to throw a rock in New England during the summer without hitting a writers' conference. For a decade the Bennington Writing Workshops proved wildly successful and oversubscribed; students wanted, for good and sufficient reason, to come and sit at the feet of those who came to teach, and I've named only the enduring dead because those living writers who joined us are legion and because the workshop too has died. There's too much competition and too little local motivation; my successors as directors of the program have turned their attention elsewhere; Rest in Peace.

This, then, is a Requiem for a Writers' Conference—for all those vivid days and nights, those years in which we ate and drank and smoked and argued and embraced the very stuff of poetry and prose, those summer parties on the lawn and children on the swingsets and classes full, it seemed, of consequence: the discovery of talent and the dear dream it might thrive.

Those who work in the teaching profession would, I think, agree with me that it's an honorable calling; the transmission of craft tips such letters contain need not be overrated but should not be dismissed. It's not nothing that we do. Time after time the flattery of imitation will alter and enlarge to emulation; then emulation in its turn becomes originality. We copy and we borrow (a descant here, a harmony there) until our own voice issues as a collective intonation and (if we be fortunate) chorale. The regret-filled reward for a teacher—or so Dante suggests it might have been for Virgil—is that moment when the guide avers: I have brought you to this distant place and now can lead no farther. Fare forward, voyager.

This last phrase—once again, according to that preternaturally aged young poet, T. S. Eliot—is the Buddha's dying valediction to his grief-stricken disciples: "Not farewell, but fare forward, voyager." And Eliot's notion of "Tradition and the Individual Talent" also feels pertinent here. What we hope our students learn to hear is in some sense an echo of the texts we studied at another's behest; the past stays current in the telling, and if I shamelessly refer to Dante and Virgil and Eliot, not to mention Gautama Buddha, it's because their music still sounds out to me in a way that makes all present song variation on a theme. What we know of Dante's Florence or Virgil's Carthage, after all, comes down to us in language, and if you remember nothing else about this letter, Franz, remember please to read. . . .

That "pride" alluded to above is, I believe, characteristic. Take any group of writers and sooner or later they'll tell you who they worked with when, who taught them what or whom they taught. And though some of this may sound like profit-sharing or mere boastfulness, it is on the whole benign. Every teacher worthy of the name takes pleasure in the success of students, and the more the merrier; to believe that the victory of X must necessarily entail the defeat of Y or Z is, I think, absurd. We have labored far too long with the imagery of Oscar night and the misleading metaphor of prizefights; art can claim no "heavyweight champ" or "knockout performance" or lone contender left in the ring; a large book enlarges us all.

Writing cannot, we are told, be taught; it must nonetheless be learned. How does one make sense of such a paradox and a seeming contradiction with which an increasing number of us live? It's easy to inveigh against the workshop "groupie" or the author who solicits opinion for the same manuscript time and again, then shifts a semicolon or excises an adjective and believes that this draft's a new draft. Not every teacher merits respectful attention and not every student improves. But the worst that's done is not much harm and the best is a good deal better than that; a culture does itself no damage by attending to its language, and often such a collocation can yield real results; the history of art is full of stories, strategies, techniques, and lessons exchanged.

"The best things come," as Henry James pronounced in his book about Hawthorne, "from the talents that are members of a group."

I have been the full-fledged student of a writer only once. John Updike is, I think, one of the most literate and able critics of our time. His breadth of reading, acuity of insight, and grace of expression must give most scholars pause; he would no doubt be welcome at any institution in any of the fifty states. But he has remained at a stiff arm's remove from Academe, and has earned his living by the pen alone. In the summer of 1962, however, his resolution wavered and he agreed to teach—at Harvard Summer School. I wanted to remain in Cambridge and therefore applied for the course. It was an offhand decision; I barely had heard of his name. When he accepted me into his fiction workshop, it would have been ungrateful to drop out.

In retrospect I see more clearly how lucky and right was that choice. The first word I wrote for Updike was the first of my first novel. Like any self-respecting undergraduate, I intended to be either a poet, a folk singer, or a movie star. I considered "prose" and "prosaic" to be cognate terms. (They are, admittedly, but I know something more by now about the other three professions and would not trade.) The young man's fancy is poetic, and his models are Rimbaud or Keats. Mine were, at any rate; my first compositions were suicide notes. But I was signed up for a writing workshop with no idea of what to write and not much time to decide. The day of that decision is vivid to me still.

A friend and I were strolling around a lake in Wellesley; we'd been reading for final exams. I heard him out as to his future; then he had to listen to me. I had tried my hand already at the shorter stuff, I said, I was going to write a novel. That was what a summer should consist of—something ambitious, no piddling little enterprise like Chekhov's but something on the scale of, let's say, *Moby-Dick*. Yet before I wrote my masterpiece I had to plan it out. What do first novels consist of? I asked—then answered, nodding sagely at a red-haired girl in a bikini emerging from the lake. First novels are either the myth of Narcissus or the parable of the Prodigal Son—but generally disguised. Their authors do not understand they fit an ancient mold. I already knew enough about Narcissus, I confessed, and therefore would elect the latter; I'd rewrite the parable. The difference was that my revision would be conscious—whereas most young novelists fail to see themselves in sufficiently explicit mythic terms.

This was not my problem, but there were other problems to solve. I knew nothing about the landscape of the Bible, for instance, and had to find a substitute. My friend lit a cigarette; we considered. It happened that I'd been to Greece the previous summer and traveled wide-eyed for weeks. I would replace one landscape with another. The parable has three component parts: the son leaves home, spends time away, and returns. My novel too would have three components, with Rhodes and Athens as its locales. My Greek protagonist would go from the island to the city and "eat up his substance with whores."

The girl in the bikini trailed drops of water where she walked; she shook her long hair free. I instructed my friend that hetarae in Athens had FOLLOW ME incised backwards on their sandals, so that they could print directions in the dust. She rounded a bend in the path. The question of contemporaneity engaged me for three minutes. I knew enough about modern-day Greece to fake it, possibly, but knew I'd never know enough about the ways of antique Attica; the prostitute's sandal exhausted my lore. It would take much less research to update the parable. So there, within ten minutes, I had it: a contemporary version of the parable of the Prodigal Son that followed the text faithfully and yet took place in Greece. The rest was an issue of filling in blanks; I started to, next week.

I have told this tongue-in-cheek, but it is nonetheless true. The epigraph of *The Martlet's Tale* is the first line of the parable; the great original is buried in my version, phrase by phrase. I revised the novel many times and by the time I'd finished was no longer a beginner. Looking back I'm astonished, however; it all fell so neatly in place. An editor at Lippincott ushered me into his office and agreed to bring out the book. "You're a very fortunate young man," he said, but I thought his politeness routine. I took success for granted when it came. My photograph in magazines seemed merely an occasion for judging the likeness; a long and flattering review in *The New York Times* on publication day was no more than an author expected; I ate expensive lunches with the cheerful certainty that someone else would pay.

In some degree, moreover, this very blindness worked to my advantage. I had been accustomed to a schoolboy's notion of success and would have dealt with failure far less equably. Had Updike not encouraged me, I cannot say for certain if I would have persevered; there were many windscraps in the wind, and I followed the favoring breeze. Harvard does prepare you for the world in this one crucial way: if you succeed within those walls you assume that you will when outside. When I handed in *The Martlet's Tale*'s first chapter, and my teacher's reaction was praise, I concluded that the rest must follow as the night does day. I suppose I stood out in his class; I certainly tried to; his wary approval meant much. I wrote a second chapter and was hooked.

So now we turn from memory to its kissing cousin, desire. What I would like to tell you, Franz, is how much it meant and means to me to conjure language out of air, to lie for a living and with a straight face. Too, "meant" and "means" provide a kind of continuity ("strange convention of critical discourse," as my first paragraph suggests), the past tense becoming the present and its own refrain. The word itself is double-edged: as an imperative "refrain" means *stop*; as a component part of verse it means, instead, *repeat*.

Freud called art "socially validated daydreaming," and the definition, though ungenerous, is apt; I rise early every morning and let out the dog or in the cat and make myself a cup of coffee and sit down to make things up. What I hope for you, my friend, is some version of the pleasure I continue to derive when words edge up against each other in a way that makes them vivid, when the *trompe l'oeil* of engaged imagination makes black marks on a blank page resemble, somehow, reality. Had I instead written "black marks on a white page," for example, the opposition of "black" and "white" would be cognate to but categorically dissimilar from my chosen "black" and "blank." In the first instance the "category" is color, and there's the formulaic juxtaposition of those old wranglers, black and white; in the second it's orthography with perhaps a nod to euphony, the *sound* of black and blank. But how strange to believe that it matters and to sit for twenty minutes while the coffee cools and dawn accretes, attempting to decide. . . .

There's a concomitant danger, of course, and you should know that too. "Whom the gods wish to destroy," writes Cyril Connolly, "they first call promising." To stand after four hours of sitting with a paragraph you know to be poor is a strange and particular torture; to feel in your bones that your best is not good enough can harrow the hardiest soul. There is much about this business that simply isn't fun.

Almost by definition the young writer models himself on those who succeed; those who fail aren't ours to emulate or read. And your first or fifth book finished merely means you must work at the second or sixth. Though I intend this letter as encouragement and want you, Franz, to stay the course, I don't want to delude you as to the charm of our profession or reward of a career; it dwindles more often than not.

"Promise," Connolly concludes, "is that dark spider with which many writers are now wrestling in obscurity and silence."

Last summer I finished a novel, a book that took me years to write, and sent it off in the mail. Then came that weary period of something like convalescence, a strange postoperative pause in which the patient's open to infection and must rest. I kicked the ground a lot and washed the same dishes over and over and rearranged my paperclips and answered the phone at first ring. Mostly it was private time and mostly my own problem, but the symptoms are peculiar and it helps to describe the disease.

John Fowles claims to loathe the day a manuscript is sent off to the publisher because then the people one has loved and lived with cease to be one's own alone and become what they actually are: inert cultural objects for others to appraise. The printed text is, after all, just an arrangement of letters, not fancy's flesh and bone.

People are inclined to think one is pleased, proud, relieved, but that seems rarely the case. It's a form of postpartum depression, perhaps, or what we're told is the captive's anxiety when released to open air. To use a third such comparison, it's a little like the amputee's conviction that there's a phantom limb: we may have lost a foot or arm, but our nerve endings register such absence as a presence nonetheless.

I saw the writer Annie Dillard earlier that same week. As soon as she heard I'd finished the book, she asked, "Are you all right?" The answer was, "No, not really," and I've been puzzling as to why: why should a more or less rational adult feel, instead of satisfied, bereft?

Partly it's a sense, I think, of the limit of attainment: that brilliant perfect thing we dreamed of looks stumblebum and second-rate from first to final page. While we were dreaming, it was back-lit, seductive; in the harsh glare of finality, the writer sees each error, each failure of nerve or technique. Imagination falters, enthusiasm wanes. And partly it's a sense of how attention wanders, how there are new stories to tell. Here's one:

I wasn't born in this country, came to it with my family when young. And for what I think was our first visit to New England, we went to Wellfleet, Massachusetts, on the outer edge of Cape Cod. I don't think I was eight years old, don't think we stayed a week. But I do remember the hotel and the walk down to the harbor and a certain whiff of marsh grass and the circling gulls: the place was called Holiday House and it must have failed to please my parents since we stayed only once. Nor is there such an establishment as the Holiday House in the village of Wellfleet today.

As it happens, however, my wife's family calls that village home, and we have a house there now and spent what I think of as my convalescence on the Cape. Someone recommended a restaurant, and I walked in to reserve a table and the place felt familiar. I'd had no reason, earlier, to visit, and an adult's vantage is different than a child's. Yet there was no mistaking the lobby, the floorboards, the configuration of what had once been our hotel; the sea wrack and the slanting light endured.

The vestibule was empty, but I heard a vacuum cleaner and followed the track of the sound. In the dining room a woman cleaned a rug. She had her back to me; she was stout and wearing a bandana and paid no attention while I coughed. So I said "Excuse me" once or twice, then asked a question loudly as to the likelihood of food that evening in this untenanted room.

When finally she sensed me, she made sounds that were not language, were the proof that she could neither hear nor speak. We stood there, staring at each other, and I swear I saw it all again—the roses by the doorway more than forty years before, the Labrador puppy that waited for scraps, the high bright sky, the wheeling birds, my dead mother vividly alive once more—till I *knew* my book was finished and the woman bent back to her work.

Max Eastman was in his eighties when I was in my twenties. We met on Martha's Vineyard and grew close; he was tolerance incarnate, with an amused abiding sense of how youth preens. I postured; I was working on a book (*Grasse 3/23/66*) that was recondite in the extreme. I'd labor in an ecstasy of self-congratulation, producing perhaps a hundred words a day, intoning the sybillant syllables until they appeared to make sense. One such passage, I remember, contained a quotation from Villon, a description of Hopi burial rites, an anagram of the name of my fifth grade teacher, an irrefutable refutation of Kant, glancing reference to Paracelsus, suggestive ditto to my agent's raven-haired assistant, paraphrase of Cymbeline's dirge, and an analysis of the orthographic and conceptual disjunction between Pope and Poe. I took my time; I let it extend to ten lines. That night I brought my morning's triumph to Max and permitted him to read. He did so in silence. He tried it aloud; so did I. When he said it made no sense and I explained the sense it made, he looked at me with generous exasperation. "Sure," he said. "That's interesting. Why don't you write it down?"

So what I hope you focus on is some particular aspect of our shared craft: a problem you first set and then attempt to solve. The distinction, say, between a simple sentence and complex. Or long and short. A sentence that is one and one that isn't. Or let us consider the distinction between a chiasmus and an oxymoron, and if you cannot at this stage distinguish the one from the other you should learn at least a little about the freedom within limits that is the system of syntax, that provides us, as it were, with the art of subjugation, so that we may begin to winnow what matters from what fails

to, what should properly take precedence in the artist's own
and chosen hierarchical arrangement—for art *is* hierarchical,
a continual adjudication of what is central and tangential, a
way of saying this matters and that doesn't, or at any rate it
matters to *me* enough to study and then set it down and my
whole course of study will therefore be to make it hereafter
and by dint of various manipulations matter to you equally—as others have done to and for me before, as you in your
turn will presumably do, because it isn't simple, is it, to return
to that bittersweet or enormously small issue of the oxymoron and, enormously bittersweet and small as the distinction might be, chiasmus, or more important, to argue in this
present age and context that such a distinction might matter,
that we should give a good goddamn or, provided that this
volume can include an even more direct and *pittoresque* alliterative conjunction, a flying fuck—for, although I'll close (not
a minute too soon, you seem to be saying, not a sentence or
a phrase too few) with the opposite assertion it is no doubt
also apposite to asseverate that art is play and cheerfulness
keeps breaking through, although admittedly of course and
in this narrow compass there are many issues we've not even
brought to the table, let alone dissected (note, please, the
metaphor implicit in such a figure and soon to be rendered
explicit, the comparison of "issues" to a thing to be dissected,
a putatively cadaverous—what, cat? skeleton? frog in
formaldehyde? fetal pig?—because for me in aging memory
it's back and forth again to *Das Ding an sich* if not as yet
thingliness, thingsomeness, and although there are writers
unnumbered who construe their work to be issue oriented,
your 'umble servant does not number himself without reservation among them, hoping only and again, again, to make a
thing of beauty and to link that non-Euclidean shape with its
near-equivalent, truth), so much we've failed to mention
about the marketplace, the pleasures of collegiality or hor-
rors attendant on careerism, the contours of a long career as
opposed to, by contrast, a short, and there is so much more to
say and though good master Pope averred "And ten low

words oft creep in one dull line," I think it's time now to embrace simplicity and stop.

Forgive me, Franz; I've grown as runic and oracular as that fellow who harangued you almost a century since. What it comes down to both at the end and in the beginning is work. In the beginning was the work and work and work. There are many and elegant ways *not* to write, but the definition of a writer is, simply, "one who writes."

And let me also repeat the definition that caused my uncle to declare, "Not bad," the tag line from Rilke's sustained piece of prose, *The Notebooks of Malte Laurids Brigge*. It seems to me a talisman, a phrase to tack above the writing desk or underneath the pillow:

"He was a poet. Which is to say, he despised the inexact."
Leben sie wohl, friend. Take care.

A Prayer for the Daughters

When our first daughter had her first—as I persisted in calling him—"gentleman caller," I harrumphed about the house and was imperious and difficult. More so than usual, even. I grumbled over unwashed glasses in the sink, complained about the way the two of them left our living room in disarray, noted the way the fellow failed to volunteer assistance while I mowed the lawn. Better still, he could have offered to mow it himself and then take out the trash and wash my car and rotate the tires. Finally a friend—the dedicatee of this volume—taped the following instruction to our refrigerator door: BE KIND TO YOUNG PETER.

It hadn't occurred to me, really; I thought young so-and-so should instead be kind to *me*. Surely *I* was the one who required attention and merited constant concern. What

happened, I asked my long-suffering wife, to the expectation of manners, the old habits of propriety and formal
address; why did he call me "Nick," not "Sir"?

"What happened is you have daughters," she said, "and
the rules have changed."

She was right, of course, she's always right, and I try to
be kind to young Peter or Paul. I was raised in a family with
only sons, and we have only daughters, and the rules have
changed. What my parents took for granted—an unques-
tioning if wholly external obedience, a sense that children
should be seen not heard, and then not until their faces were
scrubbed—is no longer ours to take. And what my parents'
parents took for granted—an equivalence of race, creed, class
amounting nearly to an "arranged" or "brokered" marriage—is the exception now, not the rule.

The fellow who so famously killed King Laius at a crossroads got to sleep with Mummy as reward. It didn't turn out
all that well for Oedipus, of course, but for some years in
Thebes he was very much respected and obeyed. When *he*
suggested to his subjects that they mow the lawn or wash
the car they made themselves useful, I'm sure. Yet his coun-
terpart, Electra, had a harder time of it; she and her brother
Orestes did away with their mother and wicked stepfather
in order to revenge dear Dad, not to share his bed. And then
there were all those Furies to contend with, all that atoning
to do. . . .

Freud writes of this, it seems to me, with a kind of clear-
eyed confusion: the Electra complex has been less celebrated
in our culture than the Oedipus. The "mother's boy" has
been widely assessed, the "father's daughter" less so. Might
this not be the case, perhaps, because Dr. Freud and his wife
had six children, of whom the famous one is Anna, who carried on as guardian of his work? So the parable becomes
instead the story of Lot with his salt daughters or Lear and
Cordelia alone in the cell, chatting cheerfully, playing patty-
cake and holding each other, "God's spies."

I'm not being fair here, obviously, and write this tongue-in-cheek. I've donned the robes of Old Mr. Curmudgeon in order to make an obvious point: the parent-child relationship has altered over time. Altered also with the teller's vantage, and mine should be located so that the reader may triangulate perspective—taking a reading, as it were, on the writer's point of view. My own is that of a father who, when young, did what he could to alienate the affections of other men's daughters from their own fathers and must school himself to like it now while others do the same. . . .

I do; I like it very much; I've been gracefully instructed in the pleasures of paternity by Francesca Barbara Delbanco and Andrea Katherine Delbanco, now twenty-three and nineteen. In 1985 (our daughters then were eleven and seven) I published an autobiographical essay that contains this paragraph. I'm struck, in fact, by how little has changed—or, rather, by the way what changes is but surface alteration. Deep currents stay the course.

So here is the opening snapshot of this brief family album:

Of late our life is located, and we travel when we can. It's a rushed tranquility, a hurried standing still. Friends die, divorce, remarry, retire, make headlines, quarrel, get fat. The children grow. As one of three sons I find it a daily instruction to be the father of daughters instead. Cesca is meditative, inward—a literate person with poise. She has humor, self-assurance and wants to be an actress. . . . Andrea had a dislocated hip at birth and spent months in a remedial brace, then a cast. Released, she has rocketed everywhere—a passionate, spark-sending imp. I work at home and am distracted often, am often forgetful, abrupt. But I want to take advantage of this moment, these crossroads, the page— want to write what they anyhow know. Their parents love them very much. They are luminous presences, each.

Our elder child came wailing to this world in Cambridge, New York, an upstate village with a hospital so small that she and her mother, Elena, made up the entire population of the maternity ward. I was teaching at Bennington College, fifteen miles across the border in Vermont. Francesca was born on a Sunday, May 26, and my first scheduled class that week took place on Tuesday morning. "Poetic Drama and Dramatic Poetry" was a course in which we focused on those poets (Dylan Thomas, Samuel Beckett, T. S. Eliot, and others) who in this century were also writing plays. What interested *me*, at least, was how a poet throws his voice—how the lyric intensity of first-person utterance changes timbre when the "I" is someone else. Dramatic monologue gives way to drama when the monologue enlarges into dialogue, or so I told my students, and the fine line between them is one we as audience must try to draw.

In Bennington such seminars took place, often as not, in the living rooms of student dorms, and there was unforced informality to the way we met, sat, talked. My students knew about my daughter's birth before I arrived to announce it; in such a community news travels fast. Our final author for the term was William Butler Yeats, whose poetry and verse plays we were studying as the spring wore on. So it seemed right and fitting to offer a toast; I read, at the start of the session, "A Prayer for My Daughter." And brought champagne to class.

I remember it clearly: the overstuffed chairs, the morning light on yellow walls, the stained carpet and the plastic cups and crackers and pretzels and peanuts and cheese. " 'Once more the storm is howling,' " I began, " 'and half-hid, under this cradle-hood and coverlid my child sleeps on.' " Yeats writes of "the great gloom that is in my mind" and avers that women should be apolitical, subservient—a strange sort of prayer to read nowadays, but commanding then as now in its shapely, stately form. He dated the poem June 1919, and we talked about what changes the ensuing years had wrought. Then we proceeded through the pieties, the poet's canny wish that his daughter should be beautiful but not with an excessive "beauty to make a stranger's eye distraught," the hope that she would prove "a flourishing hidden tree" and "be happy still" in the world's "windy quarter." That great rhetorical question of the last stanza—"How but in custom and in ceremony are innocence and beauty born?"—seemed its own answer to us all, and at the ringing final assertion, "Ceremony's a name for the rich horn, and custom for the spreading laurel tree," the students stood and cheered.

It had been a hard spring for me; my mother had died that same March. She knew about the pregnancy and gave a hands-on blessing to Elena, although she did not live to see the child who would receive her name. In ways that still astonish her parents, our daughter resembles my mother: the skin, the shape, the right foot slightly splayed while walking, the quality of impatient intelligence and sharp wit all argue a sort of transmission. She dislikes bugs and birds the way my mother did; she likes the same perfume. If there be such a thing as soul and if souls might transmogrify, then something of the sort has happened here. And though I did not know it then, my mother's death and daughter's birth would fuse in the heart's calendar; I cannot date the one without recollecting the other.

It's a universal story; the wheel circles for us all. "Whatever is begotten, born, or dies"—to quote another of the poet's famous plaints—reminds us, or ought to, "Of what is past, or passing, or to come." Our toddlers are gracious young women today, and both of them live elsewhere. As do we. I no longer teach at Bennington, and Elena and I have not returned to that hospital in Cambridge for more than twenty years. The house we took Francesca to (swaddled in blankets, sweating in the late-May heat) has been long since sold; the blue spruce I planted to commemorate her birthday is thirty feet high and the new owners' problem when it sheds needles on the entrance path; the doctor who delivered her has also moved away. The nurses have no doubt retired, and those who were my students then are parents now themselves. But it takes little effort to set that morning's scene again: the sunlight on the carpet, the young people silent in the room, the ice chest and cold-beaded bottles of Mumms, the proud father reading William Butler Yeats, half-drunk and wholly elated, reciting "may she live like some green laurel rooted in one dear perpetual place."

What's rooted is memory; what's perpetual are—great definition of the poet's work—"magnanimities of sound"; what we carry where we wander is the spoor of where we've been. So now that I am older than was Yeats himself when he prayed for his girl, and now that I too may proclaim what I wish for my daughter, our daughters, I'm happy to comply.

But first, a disclaimer. Art is exactness, the naming of names, and I have no thoughts worth writing down that could properly be called abstract. The "smiling public man" Yeats called himself when among schoolchildren could be distracted readily by dancers and the "brightening glance"; he distrusted the political asseveration. So do I. The notion that fathers of the present day bear a separate relation to their daughters than they did a century or six ago is no doubt accurate; it does not, however, engage me. Patterns of obedience and imitation, matters of preserved virginity and the size of dowries and same-sex partnership and professional aspiration and liberated ambition—all these are more important to the sociologist than the novelist. An overview provided by statistics or schematics is beside the present point.

I want to write these lines since they limn for me a particular case: I am a father who has daughters, and language is a form of prayer for those with faith in articulate art. Or, to misappropriate Claudius—that lethal stepfather in the great poetic drama by the greatest of our English dramatists and poets—"My words fly up; my thoughts remain below." The usurper's on his knees, and praying, and he admits at soliloquy's end that he has failed to find salvation. In *Hamlet*, of course, this describes the king's weakness; I prefer, however, to think of all such wordy earthbound striving as an essay or assay of strength. . . .

And authors—or, at any rate, this particular one—work at home. Almost by professional definition we witness and can daily participate in and thereafter report on our own children's progress; we are more a part of process in the domestic venue than those fathers who earn livelihoods in factory or field. Look for the wayfaring dad in the daycare center or fetching daughters after school and you'll find, it well may be, a poet between stanzas or a novelist at chapter's break. Too, it seems to me that the absence of hired help in most American households has eradicated distance in a way that ramifies: change your daughter's diapers often enough and you're not likely to be curtseyed to in the drawing room.

I mean by this that the rotogravure ideal of the Victorian or Edwardian gentleman reading papers by the fireplace and noddingly receiving the day's-end account from the governess as to his children's deportment is almost wholly obsolete; Mary Poppins doesn't do the cooking or the cleaning anymore. Those TV situation comedies that feature the family unit now seldom have a maid—or if they do, the serving role is powered by nostalgia, the "downstairs" turning tables on the "upstairs" while the table's being set. Charles Dickens, Victor Hugo, James Joyce, Leo Tolstoi, Thomas Mann, and Mark Twain—to name only a few authorial "authority" figures with daughters—did not to my knowledge make peanut-butter sandwiches or strip beds. And even when Tolstoi near the end of his life embraced simplicity and insisted on sweeping out his parlor, it was not for the sake of a child. These six men span a century and six different countries, but they have in common a privileged aloofness from domestic chores. We may harrumph and grumble, as I do in this essay's opening paragraph, but the yield of such proximity far far outweighs the cost.

"In courtesy I'd have her chiefly learned," writes Yeats, and means by this "the old high ways"—half Castiglione, half coquette. His anger at Maud Gonne seems unattractive here; fine women need not eat "a crazy salad with their meat," or if they choose to do so, need not therefore be labeled insane. What's "peddled in the thoroughfares" as he in his poetical exasperation claims, "are arrogance and hatred"; this is, it scarcely need be said, a constricting and constricted view of women's earned place in the world. But I have to admit to a more than sneaking sympathy for Yeats's wish, and like to think young ladies nearing the millennium need not be wholly ignorant of what was meant by "courtesy"—that our daughters will have suitors and that their suitors will send flowers and hold open doors. I recognize, of course, that this is retrograde if not reactionary, but I was raised in a family where manners mattered, and my formidable grandmother had no greater praise for her grandson than to call him "my chevalier." Men left the room to smoke cigars; they stood when she rose from her chair.

So it does seem to me that something has been sacrificed to the ideal of practical equality, lost to our liberated sisterhood while so much else is gained. In many ways, I'd guess, it's more difficult to be a woman now than was the case before, and more daunting a challenge to be both female and professional than is the case for men; the job description's broader and the task more various. That scarifying Teutonic definition of a woman's work, *Küchen, Kirchen, Kinder,* had one virtue only—simplicity—and now that the triad enlarges beyond kitchen, church, and children the equation grows complex. This has been widely noted and reported on, and I veer perilously close to those gender generalizations I promised to avoid. But it's specific, really; I pray our daughters flourish both at home and in the world. May they manage and rest easy with that problematic conjunction of the public and the private life; may they find pleasure and fulfillment turn by turn in each.

In one way or another, we compose such prayers often. In the beginning was the word, and every daughter in my fiction has been created in the image of my actual daughters. Or, to extend the metaphor, these portrayals may be read as sketches done from life. I don't mean by this, of course, that Francesca and Andrea have been characters I've written— even in a nonfiction account of our family's time together abroad (*Running in Place: Scenes from the South of France*) I gave them lines they never spoke and attitudes they did not entirely espouse. But here, from *Stillness*, a novel I published in 1983, is an articulated prayer that the father of the Sherbrooke children enters in his journal. His hopes are mine.

March 25. Temperature at six o'clock, forty-two degrees. No wind. I drink my coffee peaceably; train prompt. . . . May my son know just such peace, and may my daughter grow up beloved. It is a worldly prayer but the single thing I pray. Harriet and Judah. May their manners be courtly yet frank. May they have physical health, and long life, and sufficient comeliness to please the eye but not bedazzle. May their learning be solid not showy, and their skills precise. May his work engage him; may they multiply. Let them continue in this house, as I have continued, and after their departure may they welcome the thought of return.

There is much in these lines that echoes Yeats, and consciously—the wish that the children prove "courtly yet frank," the hope for "sufficient comeliness to please the eye but not bedazzle," and the desire that the children "continue in this house . . . and welcome the thought of return." My fictive wild old wicked man does not exist, nor do Harriet and Judah Sherbrooke except insofar as they live on the page, but in that alchemy with which all authors are familiar I found myself able to dream about my own two children while inventing his.

Such transposition is routine; we write out of experience, but experience includes the act of writing and incorporates Yeats's notion of the antiself or mask. Although I come from a household of sons, my offspring are female and each has a sister. The terms of sibling rivalry or mutual supportiveness are therefore different, and the terms of aspiration also change. No matter how assiduously we worked to eradicate gender-specific behavior, our girls hoped to be ballerinas, not baseball players; they preferred finery to fishing and shrieked at a mouse. And though it embarrasses me to admit this, I still feel somehow *useful* when summoned from my desk to squash a bug or carry a spider outside; when asked by them to lift something heavy or fix something broken I feel honored by their confidence that I can carry, lift, fix.

May their learning be solid not showy, and their skills precise, my fictive father prays. In this regard also I share his hopes and have labored hard; unnumbered hours of homework, of visits to museums and bookstores and concert halls have been logged in the ledger called "learning"; my wife and I have been committed to the notion of instructedness as another set of parents might teach survival skills. Our daughters have had no lessons in what we used to call "Home Ec.," or the finishing schools called "deportment," but they can tell the difference at fifty paces easily between the real cultural thing and the fraud; I confidently expect for them both an ongoing life of the mind. The idea that "school" can be "finished" has had no currency at home. And the one rider I'd attach to my fond fictive parent's wish is that he now would also say, *May her work engage her,* since no present father dares to think his daughter need not work.

So, yes, I am conditioned by tradition. "And may her bridegroom bring her to a house," the poet writes, and however limited or patriarchal it seems I find myself in sympathy with that future-facing desire. Yes, I want my daughters to walk at some point down some aisle on my arm—though I don't require them to wear white or be married in a building that has aisles. Yes, I want them to be happy in the way their parents have been, and to emulate as women that exemplary woman who nurtured them throughout their youth and continues to do so today. I recognize that married love is neither original nor, perhaps, now fashionable—but it has made their father happy for nearly thirty years. And what I hope for them is not something other or contrary but, rather, more of the same.

These verbs *want* and *hope* are not, I trust, imperatives; neither, come to that, is the verb *trust*. Deploy them here as nouns instead, as the conditions of trust and hope and the explicit parental desire to keep children free from want. I would feel the same way about sons if we had had them, would treat them in the same way—in terms of both the expectation and the assessment of what's been achieved. But this is moot; I cannot tell; I can only report on the actual. That "Horn of Plenty" to which Yeats refers—and which he in anger at Maud Gonne transforms to "an old bellows full of angry wind"—pours out upon our table when our daughters sit at it, and the sum and substance of my prayer is that this may continue, not change.

A decade ago, from *Running in Place*, these lines:

Andrea likes to draw. Each morning we gather flowers, arrange them in a vase, and scrupulously she copies what she sees. I work outside, on the tile patio, and she joins me there in the second wicker chair. She has a drawing pad and watercolors and Caran d'Ache crayons and pencils in ranked rows; she places the vase on the table and outlines it lightly in pencil, then fills in the shape.

"Why don't you draw the step?" I say. "Those steps there, by the table."

She shakes her head.

"Why don't you make it blue?"

"It isn't."

"It could be."

"Not this step, Daddy. It's orange."

"If you made it blue it would look that way to anyone who saw the picture."

"They'd be wrong," she says.

"Don't be so certain, darling. How do you know what that painter was seeing—the one we looked at yesterday—when he painted castles. Maybe he was dreaming them."

"He wasn't."

"Maybe he dreamed them so clearly that all these years later we see what he saw the day he shut his eyes."

"This step is orange," she says.

Other parents dote on and record their progeny with cameras and tape recorders and video cassettes. Predictably enough, my own form of retention was to write an annual letter to each of our children on or near their birthdays, reporting on the things they'd done and learned. These epistles bulk large in the daybook, and I don't propose to quote from them at length. But here's a sample from the first such letter after the first anniversary of Francesca's birth:

May 29, 1975. . . . You know which one's your nose, though tend to poke your cheek or mouth when we ask you to find it; you can stand a lot more steadily than you pretend, and, when distracted, do so for a minute at a time. You love to dance and shimmy, love to clap your hands when asked how big you are (eliminating as indecorous by now the infant game of raising hands when asked how big is Cesca, since you've got that trick down pat). You think, as do the rest of us, you're lovely to look at, and take most any opportunity to do so—in toasters in particular, or spoons, and the house sprouts mirrors for your special pleasure. Also gates, since you're a wanderer with splinters in your knees to attest to my incompetent floor-sanding. . . .

Here's an extract from a letter to Andrea Katherine Delbanco, turning three:

March 15, 1981. . . . Tootsie Rolls. Last August when we were in England it was Granny Piggott's candy, and there've been intermittent passions for bubble gum and lollypops and cookies and the like. But you're a faithful devotee, the Tootsie Roll kid queen; you fall asleep clutching one in the folds of what you still call "blankety" and wake hunting one on the instant. (You don't do much of the former, byethebye—sleeping, I mean—and you're wakefulness incarnate by seven at the latest every day.) We draw pictures of them, sequester them in pockets and plastic bags—and, splendidly, you asked for a Tootsie Roll cake for your birthday. Also a Benjy sleeping bag, much to your tasteful parents' distress. But when Mommy pointed to the selection in the Sears catalogue several weeks later, hoping you'd have forgotten, you proved as avid and exact a file cabinet for memory as is your big sister. "I told you already," you announced, with that magisterial impatience you've learned since first attended to by an anxious, waiting world. . . .

Time now to shelve the family album and go out and mow the lawn. Time now to admit that "prayer" comes hard to one whose mode is secular, and superstitious at that; mostly what I hoped for has been granted and mostly what I wish for is that it can be retained. Not preserved in amber or even in such language as this but via that alkahest, memory, so that what was past and passing may remain in what's to come.

For years we were inseparable as a quartet, going everywhere together and sharing one roof. Now time and the river have done their slow work, and we're together only rarely and on prearranged occasions. This is as it should be. But always still, as soon as possible—and it delights their parents always—the two of them go off together and, from behind their shared closed door, the sound of laughter comes. "Be kind to young Peter," they say. . . .

What I pray now for my daughters is that they will have children whose fathers admire them as much as I do mine. And what I pray for those children is that their mothers prove as splendid a mother as is and has been their own. I want them safe. I want them healthy, not ill or at risk. I want them protected from want. I mean them to know what they mean.

Less and More

As my title suggests, this essay deals with linkage and could well have been called "More and Less." Or "Less or More" or "More is Less"; it's the conjunction of the words I wish to focus on, not the disjunction between them: two comparative terms in one breath. "More or less" is the common expression, of course—a way of indicating approximate accuracy—and it approximates my meaning, as does the aesthetic pronouncement, so famous in our modern age, that "less is more." The point, at least provisionally and at least for openers, is that "less and more" belong together; they've been joined at the titular hip.

And the burden of these pages will be to reverse expectation—so that "more" need not loom larger in its hierarchical connotation than "less." We build our structures from the bottom up; the narrow apex of a triangle requires the broad base. The "crowning glory" of a cupola or spire would have little value or importance at ground level, and managerial techniques now emphasize the lateral, not vertical, arrangement; the superannuated executive will likely get "kicked upstairs." Yet we "strip down for action" and "get down to brass tacks"; parable and fable both insist that the higher we tower the harder we fall. According to the story, a bending reed outlasted the storm that killed a mighty oak. Time and again in the natural world the diminutive creature surpasses the large; the dinosaur is but a memory, whereas cockroaches endure.

Sideways motion equally may represent advance. Not all progress is predictable or regular; change comes in fits and starts. Nor is the ranking absolute; the terms aren't "most and least." So perhaps our proper figure is not a triangle or pyramid but a circle or sphere. The mighty rolling wheel of industry and the engines of advancement could be drawn instead as Fortune's Wheel, with a cautionary warning that the prosperous will come undone and the proud man topple. If it's true that what goes up comes down and that every action engenders a reaction, then the dialectic offers us our dance step: one forward, one back, sideways slide. We start dying with the newborn's breath, and Shakespeare's "second childhood"— the last stage of the pilgrimage described in *As You Like It*— replicates the first. Perhaps the wheel's hub, spoke, and rim are one within this turning world: both less and more amounting not so much to progress as to the zero sum.

Last winter I made a quick trip to that southwest portion of Vermont I called, for decades, home. It was ice-riddled, bone-chillingly cold, and not easy to negotiate the hills. But one of the things that I did on the trip was pay a visit to a friend, a woman now nearly a hundred years old, who'd been immobilized by snow; she told me that for six weeks running she'd left the house only to go the doctor or when someone offered to drive.

Those offers come infrequently; she's in an old people's home. It's a common story: widowhood, infirmity, then the doctor's strong suggestion that she shouldn't live alone. Next a couple of falls in a bathtub and the collective decision that supervised living is best. Her large family has long ago moved elsewhere; her children are themselves too old to care for her properly, her grandchildren otherwise engaged, her great-grandchildren too young. There are seventeen of them, by recent count, and the inexorable arithmetic of population—a kind of exponential increase derived from that aged single stem. There's a family photograph propped by her bed in which she sits surrounded by some thirty-odd descendants, all smiling, all saying "Cheese."

I'm not one of them, not a relative. But in absolute terms she matters to me and my wife; she took care of our two daughters way back when. We've been close for twenty years. So I try not to go to that part of the world without stopping by to visit, to bring her news and flowers and wave the gossip flag. For though her physical agility has lessened, though she walks with a cane and uses a hearing aid, there's no real diminution of her mental faculties: this woman— let's call her Harriet—is tack-sharp still. She wants to be out in the world.

And after mud season it's possible; from late spring through autumn it's fine. She can visit her hairdresser, maybe, or meet a friend in a restaurant, or have a grandchild take her touring just to see the sights. But mobility's an issue in winter; the white house where they've put her sits at the top of a high hill, at the end of a long unplowed drive. And there's no money for road maintenance; the caretaker is careful with both salt and sand. He plows the place from time to time—enough to make certain that he can get out. That's about it, however, and few others manage: the five old people interred in the house drink soup and masticate sandwiches and sit and sleep and watch television and, outside, the snow.

So I take my rented car and barrel through. The doorbell is broken, the front door unlocked. I've called ahead; she's waiting, and we settle in. "My my," she says, "you're a sight for sore eyes," but what she wants to talk about is trouble, not good news. Harriet complains about the staff, the owners, the company, the food. When she lived down in the village her house was full of visitors, and she produced the best sticky buns and oyster stew from Brattleboro to Rutland. She was famous for her popovers and jam. These days she's losing weight; each night she looks down at her plate and says, "Oh no, oh, not again." Though she's precisely as old as the century, she feels like a hundred and five. She can't even go to church. She was late for her doctor's appointment last week, and when the nurse said, "Better late than never," Harriet had disagreed. "Don't blame me," she said. "When I was on my own two feet I never was a single minute late."

So I say how things are hard, how the world feels like the weather and things keep on slipping downhill. Harriet looks up at me. She shakes her white head and, swallowing, adjusts her teeth. "There's more truth than poetry in that," she says. I ask her to repeat the phrase; she does. "There's more truth than poetry in that."

Yet the currency great poets coin is truth. "Time's thievish progress to eternity," as Shakespeare wrote, feels inescapable. And most of us grow used, in one way or another, to transactions that pass the time—that mark the "thievish progress" from youth to middle age. Gain and loss are kissing cousins; it's hard to grow up without growing older, or move to a new place without leaving something behind. There are often compensations in such changes—of towns, say, or countries or consorts. You lose a child at home but get grandchildren in the neighborhood, you gain in gravity while gaining weight; you shift politics or clothing styles or jobs.

These are year-end reflections, often as not—attached to that Grim Reaper we now call Father Time. According to the Orphics, our Hallmark notecard image of a graybeard with a blade has a more edgy origin—having to do with an oracle that warned the great god Ouranos he would be supplanted by his son. So the fierce creature ate his progeny in order to protect himself, as in Francisco Goya's nightmarish image of that bearded Titan swallowing his seed. But Mother Gaea hid and saved her best-beloved Kronos, serving up a rock for Ouranos to eat. When Kronos grew up, and up to the job, he took a scythe and cut off his father's genitals, thereby assuming dominion—at least until his own boy Zeus did much the same. This Greek parable was adopted by the Romans with an adaptive spelling change; Kronos is spelled with a K, but they recorded it as Chronos instead. This latter spelling has to do with the Greek root for "time," as in chronology, chronometry, etc., so the ambitious boy got transmuted in the telling to graybeard Father Time. And that's what the Grim Reaper really means and why he wields a sickle, and what he slices off—not the green stalk of the old year, since in our northern latitudes not much grows in December.

When a doctor says, "You must take these pills; you must stop smoking or drinking or start to wear a pacemaker," we tend to take such injunctions seriously indeed. When an employer says "You're fired" or the voting public votes you out of office or a manager tells you you won't make the team, it's food for remedial thought. There are happy occasions for change also, of course, and these are the ones that we tend to call progress: we win the lottery or pennant, we get selected by Publisher's Clearing House to take a vacation in Tahiti, we discover that an ice cream flavor we patented ten years ago is now the nation's rage. . . .

Most of the time, however, our life shifts are less seismic—a little sideways motion, a small alteration of emphasis, a line crossed that we fail to notice till we're on the other side. We formalize the solstice, but winter blends to spring. We avidly look forward to the annual office party, then one year come to think of it as an annual bore. A new job, a new coat grows old. The child who scrutinizes his or her daily reflection in the mirror cannot see how large a change the year-end visitor perceives: "How much you've grown," shrieks Aunt Elsie or Uncle Bert, while inwardly the object of their enthusiasm shrinks. Time-lapse photography has made of change an art form: plants thrust up from the frozen earth, unfold, flower, and fade and disappear in compressed extended action; so too with our faces and shapes. Consider the family album: a child in nursery school, then summer camp, then at college commencement, then the twenty-fifth reunion and the eightieth birthday celebration; the passage of time is made plain.

The elders of far northern tribes go out onto the ice, I'm told, when there's insufficient food for all to live through a hard winter. Between the example of peremptory dismissal provided by young Kronos and the example of such sacrifice there must be some room to maneuver, and that's where the time-lapse pertains. As though entropy and dissolution were negative only, a forced occasion for change. Little by little, inch by inch and day by year, things alter—and that's what occasions acknowledge: a thirteenth birthday, a twenty-first, a wedding anniversary, a golden jubilee. . . .

Long ago I bought and lived in and slowly remodeled a brick farmhouse not far from the place where Harriet still sits. "Rock Hill"—as it was called on old surveyors' maps—dated from 1820 or so, and it had been imposing once: Georgian, four chimneys, large-windowed, with a marble entry stoop worn concave from hard use. The years had rearranged but not treated it kindly; the house had the usual assortment of "improvements"—which is to say six or seven layers of wallpaper on the crumbled plaster, linoleum on the wide-planked floor, bricked-up fireplaces and fake entries and stairwells and secondary ceilings: the detritus of previous owners whose taste mirrored previous styles. Then, at the stroke of my purchaser's pen, the house became ours to renew.

Those were the days when restoration seemed less attractive than renovation; there was little in the house we wanted to preserve. My wife and I were young and ambitious, and together we gutted the place. I laid about with a sledgehammer and a wrecking bar and a good deal of enthusiasm, and soon we had what felt like the only loft within two hundred miles of Houston Street: open beams and exposed brick walls, unimpeded prospects of the stock pond and the barn, a city dweller's dream of country life. But though we could assist with what is now called "deconstruction," the reverse required skill. "Construction" was beyond our competence, so we hired carpenters to put in plate-glass windows and triple the size of the kitchen and recess the lights. The center hall, for example, acquired an iron spiral staircase; the four cramped downstairs rooms became one. It's a familiar story: by the time the structure was transformed to our entire liking we were ready to move on. Another family produced another checkbook; we shook hands and signed papers and left town.

So driving away from the old people's home, since I was in the neighborhood, I dropped by "Rock Hill" to say hello. "We're making progress with the place," the owners told me happily; "we're gaining on it. Come and see." At some point in their tenancy these people have grown obsessed with authenticity—and now they are bound and determined to restore the building to its original state. Gone our beloved spiral stairwell; returned the entrance hall. Gone our recessed floodlights; returned the candle-holder and the Argand lamp. Gone the open fireplace; returned the period mantel. They've had a harpsichord maker carve the portico; the daguerreotypes upon the walls look like last season's family portraits. Even the books on the shelves were printed in the 1820s, or before; the flowerbeds display only flowers from the first part of the last century, and when they get around to it they'll tear out the plumbing and restore the outhouse too.

Their sense of tradition is as firmly fixed, in short, as was ours of innovation, and soon there'll be no more light switches or electrical outlets or the zoned oil-fired furnace we took such pride in installing. And I felt as if I were witnessing a reel of film reversing, in which all things wound backward to the opening credits and frame. The new owners stop short of wearing costumes, but the wheel has entirely turned.

The house endures us all.

A recent study has informed us, yet again, that Americans live longer; our average life expectancy is now 76 years of age. Not long ago those digits were reversed; 67 years was what an American male could expect, and those whose memories are longer no doubt remember the number when less. It's a mixed blessing, as many have come to suspect; there's real irony in the tale of the Cumaean Sibyl, who asked for and received eternal life but forgot to ask, into the bargain, for eternal youth. And withered and shriveled away, growing older and older, uttering only the repeated despairing cry: "I want to die."

Or think of Xeno's paradox—that if we continually halve the distance toward an anticipated goal we never will attain it. There's a half left to begin with, then a quarter, then an eighth, a sixteenth, a thirty-second and so on—but the end remains, if only infinitesimally, some distance and time still ahead. In this way we approach the Sibyl's problematic immortality: if for every year of life we gain another year of life expectancy, the population changes and the terms of the problem also change.

I don't mean to engage the present debates on assisted suicide, entitlement programs, or health-care delivery, but rather to point out the obvious: our youthful solutions grow old. In important ways, I think, we need to consider what all this entails in terms of the transfer of power—how one generation prepares to make way and give over to the next. The very word "generation" suggests its own reversal; we generate and bring forth our biological replacements and get displaced and degenerate and move on. But there's a difference between doing so at age thirty and at age eighty, and most of our models are closer to the former than the latter. It's the young artist we celebrate, the young athlete and entrepreneur and politician, not to mention "model." As long as the natural course of things kept Keats or Mozart or Alexander the Great from growing old, the question of what to do with old age simply wasn't as pressing to ask. "Bodily decrepitude is wisdom," writes Yeats, but our collective wisdom on the subject seems at present scant.

We have, in America, a great many books and a good deal of advice on how to succeed, how to acquire prominence and then to maintain and increase it—instructions of all sorts on self-improvement. It's a national obsession, nearly, whether we're talking about bankbooks or golf games or biceps, whether the subject is big business or politics or entertainment or health. And such instruction manuals almost always take for granted the notion of increase and plenty, that power is ours for the taking or making, and that more will be more. The opposite—decrease, decline—is a proposition few of us focus on but all of us—consciously or no—must wrestle with, if only in terms of how to deal with what is certain: taxes, death. Just think how much more common is the usage of the meliorist word "progress" than that of its opposite, "regress"; the latter term sounds foreign and even to a degree unnatural to the American ear.

For it sometimes seems harder to give up an office than gain it, to distribute a fortune than acquire it, to retire than continue to entertain or play. Often a person is voted out of office, or gets fired or goes broke or fails to attract an audience—but these are examples of involuntary retirement. In Western civilization the idea of voluntary retirement has been almost exclusively attached to the religious life; we go behind the convent wall or kneel on the monk's cell floor to pray. The prince who chooses to be pauper does so for spiritual gain. And the answers so much a part of other cultures (the Buddhist model of renunciation, the Hindu of withdrawal) are at best an uneasy fit with present Western ways.

Imagine if the Pope chose to retire, or Queen Elizabeth

passed on the Crown to her heir apparent, or the founder of a business empire arranged an orderly transition—and the point may become more clear. Whether our national dream be that of streets paved with gold or, more modestly, a car in each garage and a chicken in every pot, the self-image of America is ineluctably linked to the idea of forward motion, the ideals of self-help, self-improvement, and self-reliance. Much of our current malaise, perhaps, can be attributed to the recognition that not all problems can be solved, not all resources are inexhaustible, frontiers cannot be pushed back without damage. "Manifest Destiny," in this reading, just means keep on keeping on. . . .

Yet Janus is a two-faced god, with eyes in front and eyes behind: the one who gives his name to January and looks both forward and back. What we require, individually and collectively, are models for that backward face: the willing withdrawal from power, learning when to say enough's enough, and how to live with less.

A number of characters in early novels—by which I mean those of the eighteenth and nineteenth centuries—have, as it were, "great expectations," or are "living on a competence" or have been left substantial or small legacies by distant uncles or maiden aunts. They don't seem to work for a living; they are eligible or marriageable in more or less direct proportion to the size of their estates. In part, perhaps, this came about because the authors of those novels would therefore need to focus less on the workaday world and could concern themselves exclusively with the inner emotional lives of their characters; if you don't spend time on the nine to five, there's more space for heart and mind. But one cannot escape the suspicion that—at least within the realm of fiction—more people used to inherit more than is the case today. Or at any rate they did so earlier; there are all those fortunate gentlemen or fortune hunters and ladies with cocked hats or dowries festooning all those pages in Austen, Balzac, and the rest.

Lately I've come to understand that this has something to do with actuarial tables; if you come into your inheritance at sixty because the maiden aunt or foreign uncle dies in their eighties or nineties it's less romantic by far. Tax laws too have altered; you can't give a kingdom away or simply designate an heir apparent and offer up the throne. Prince Charming gets long in the tooth and Cinderella gets dishpan hands if you make them wait too many years before they acquire bequests; Rumpelstiltskin could turn straw to gold, but one point of his story is that he was a bitter old man. It is, of course, the case that most of us have no inheritance or expectation of a life-altering legacy; the vast majority of people don't rely for their own living on what someone else leaves. But the novel is a middle-class art form, a description of society organized by commerce, and it's not, I think, an accident that characters with trust funds are less populous in today's pages than in those pages written two centuries ago.

Shakespeare's tragedy, *King Lear*, takes as its occasion the old man's decision, at play's start, to give up his absolute power and give everything away. He wants his children to praise and then take care of him, and according to how loudly they sing his praises he will divide his estate. Two of his daughters are hypocrites and flatter the choleric King; the youngest, who truly loves him, has nothing public to say. "Nothing comes of nothing," rages the old man famously, and what in fact comes of his decision to disinherit his darling Cordelia is general catastrophe—the madness on the heath, the kingdom in collapse. But the version I'd propose is not that Lear stay on his throne but that he offer it up to the correct daughter, in which case there'd be no trouble and, of course, no tragedy itself. It's a kind of Estate Planner's Guide, a warning about poor investments and insufficient scrutiny of the company you choose; make certain that you mean it when you allocate bequests.

What I'm trying to describe is the widespread fear—and it would seem to be the first time we as a society have felt this way—that prosperity is on the wane and not around the corner: we'll be lucky as a general rule to do as well in America as did our parents, and our children face a future less lavish than the present. In our image of the self or family or nation, the prospect of increase and plenty no longer seems to prevail. Whether the yardstick be economic or ecological, whether the enemy stands without or within, there's a sense that progress best describes the storied past and that the epoch to come will not belong to our nation as much as the era now nearly done.

Such pervasive unease may be a necessary corrective, in fact, since not all streets are paved with gold and the pot of it at rainbow's end isn't that easy to find. But think of all those heroines and heroes whose history was organized by "great expectations," and you'll see how the rising dawn of this country's great day was mirrored in, reflected by our literature. The happy ending was the rule; by now it's the exception. The girl in Rumpelstiltskin's tower too grows old with spinning, and the princess kisses an imprisoned creature who remains a frog. That "nothing comes of nothing" turns out to be, alas, the dark commercial truth.

On the French slope of the Pyrenees, beneath the high snow-crested triangular peak of Mount Canigou, stands an abbey constituted more than a thousand years ago: San Miguel de Cuxa. The names are Catalan, the monks are Benedictine, and there are very few of them remaining, five or six. They tend sheep and sell wine and cheese and peach preserves and flowers; from time to time they make visitors welcome; last month my wife and I—along with an international contingent of cellists—called the monastery home.

Cuxa has a storied history; it was founded near the village of Codalet on the 19th of June, 879. It rapidly became a place of learning, consequential disputation, and power in retreat. At the urging of Abbot Garin, the Venetian Doge Pietro Orseola journeyed west in 978 and remained in Cuxa till his death. In the eleventh century Orseola was canonized and his skull interred beneath the altar, but during his lifetime—

since he had not taken orders and could not sleep within the walls—the saint slept outside, on rock. The shape of his body, or so the locals like to say, is imprinted on the soft stone paving where the vineyard starts. Our own accommodations proved rather better: a pallet on wood planking, a cross and no mirrors on the wall, a communal bathroom three corridors away, with the only sound the monks at matins or the cellists in their practice rooms behind the low refectory where, three times a day, we ate.

There's a beautiful Lombard steeple, an eleventh-century crypt, and the remains of a grandiose cloister built in the twelfth century. That structure itself did not survive the French Revolution, or its leveling zeal in the name of equality; more than a hundred years thereafter, John J. Rockefeller gathered rocks stored in a warehouse in the region and constructed his medieval "Cloisters"—with capitals from Cuxa—on New York's Washington Heights.

In America the backward reach of history is short and, by and large, within our grasp. There are ancient buildings and burial sites on this continent also, of course, but such a structure as the Abbey of San Miguel de Cuxa is unimaginable unless purchased by a millionaire a millennium after the fact. To watch the monks trim fruit trees or the farmer spread manure, to see how snowmelt off the mountains has been channeled to the vineyards and hear the bells of grazing sheep is to witness constancy in change.

And in this time of accelerating change, of future-facing prophets and exponentially increased information, it's lovely beyond simple saying to withdraw to a place where the world is as it was. Nor did the withdrawal feel so much like a retreat as advance: the threat of invasion came only from a tourist bus, the wells had not been poisoned, and the single telephone rang in a booth in a field.

The reader will have noticed that this essay has two modes. One set of entries is personal, one impersonal; the former consists of memory and the latter of speculation. Those three descriptive anecdotes (my old friend, my old house, the Benedictine abbey that became the Cloisters) bear only a tangential relation to the straight line of "progress"; they engage it indirectly if at all. To face a ruin such as Cuxa—and, more mysteriously even, Stonehenge or the Pyramids, Uxmal or Angkor Wat—is to question in what ways we have advanced. That we have advanced as a species is self-evident, I think, and to deny this is blithely dismissive of democracy, vaccination, rockets, and our enabling technology; more people inhabit the planet with pleasure than has been the case before. The weight of progress overwhelms; the sheer density of population, traffic jams, and personal computers that herald the developed world may tempt us to turn Luddite. Yet it's a temptation we ought to resist, since only those who live in plenty yearn to live with less. . . .

Now let me use my text as test and admit that in these pages I've been more than usually allusive. Or, one might argue, elusive. I've cited Goya, Gaea, Kronos, Chronos, Father Time, the Orphics, Shakespeare, Yeats, the Luddites, and so on. And perhaps the point was made and perhaps it's memorable and perhaps there are some readers who won't think the same way again about our figurative Grim Reaper. But I'd hazard the opinion that far more will remember—or would if I wrote it well enough—the first scene about my visit to the woman in the snow. There was narrative there, a situation and dramatic sequence and an exchange in dialogue. There was not a single literary allusion, however, or quotation or citation, just a middle-aged man in a rented car who visits an old people's home. . . .

But in that passage possibly I clarified, as not elsewhere, the fact of long life and its insult to flesh, the way we are imprisoned soon or late by immobility. And this is what the novelist does, or tries to do, when making scenes: create an image of the world in words that reflects and, when we close our eyes or close the book, refracts it. If the reader can remember the woman I've called Harriet, if I have conjured her successfully, then the question of whether or not she exists, whether or when I did take that trip, whether or not she said what I report her saying, " 'There's more truth than poetry in that,' " is, or should be, moot.

The root meaning of "progress," according to *The Oxford English Dictionary*, has more to do with the physical action of movement than an abstract progressive ideal. It is, as suggested above, more literal than theoretical, more specific than abstract. The first meaning offered is "The action of stepping or marching forward or onward; onward march; journeying, traveling, travel; a journey, an expedition. (Now *rare*)."

The second definition has to do with nobility; kings and queens performed a "progress" while they made a visit of state. The third and fourth definitions have to do with "onward movement in space" and "forward movement in space" respectively, and it is only at the end of several columns of examples and several hundred years of usage that we approach the figurative definition now commonly in use: "To make progress; to proceed to a further or higher stage, or to further or higher stages continuously; to advance, get on; to develop; increase; usually to advance to better conditions, to go on or get on well, to improve continuously."

This shift from "progress" in the literal to "progress" in the figurative sense would seem to have occurred in that most hopeful of centuries, the eighteenth. Having won the Revolution and served his time as President, George Washington could write in 1796 that "Our country . . . is fast *progressing* in its political importance and social happiness" (italics mine). On the other side of the Atlantic, Mary Russell Mitford, the author of *Our Village*, would locate the term as not native: "In country towns . . . society has been progressing, (if I may borrow that expressive Americanism) at a very rapid rate." By 1850 Herbert Spencer would insist that "Progress, therefore, is not an accident, but a necessity. . . . It is a part of nature."

And the great if misrepresented scientific basis for "progress" derives, of course, from Darwin. If you accept that apes breed men and that the species *Homo sapiens* is a higher form of nature, then the whole history of evolution has to do with forward motion; we come out of the Galapagos or the Great Barrier Reef and go, sooner or later, to school. Yet it does seem to be the case that the articulated ideal of "progress" is an "expressive Americanism." Although Lord Macaulay announced in the 1830s that "The history of England is emphatically the history of progress," more often the term in its optimistic forward-facing aspect has been yoked to the New World.

But all such emphatic usage is, I think, beside the point. We should accept and celebrate the idea of diminution, of withdrawal and recurrence, as much as that of progress, so that less means, also, more. To know when to stop is as difficult—in love and business and life and warfare and environmental management and essays—as to know where to begin.

Scribble, Scribble, Scribble

"Another damned, thick, square book! Always scribble, scribble, scribble! Eh, Mr. Gibbon?" So remarked the Duke of Gloucester, in a put-down and a send-up both at once. For in this story, surely, the speaker gets the best of it, turning from his slight acquaintance bent above the desk to matters that *do* matter: the purchase of horseflesh, the Hellfire Club, the decanter of good claret. His is the sort of epigrammatic utterance to which there can be no rejoinder, the clean hit and quick-killing witticism: once over lightly and leave. . . .

But let us linger awhile. Let's first assume that the phrase is correct—that it wasn't improved in the telling, or written long after the fact. It isn't clear, however, if this formed a part of sustained conversation or an effective one-liner—if it came at the end or the start of a meeting. Was there an answer made? What might the answer have been? The jibe is formulated as a question, after all; perhaps it's a matter of mere intonation, and the rising inflection gave way to a snort. Or proffered pinch of snuff. Or inch of first-rate port.

It wouldn't work as well, of course, were Gibbon not still famous. "Scribble, scribble! Eh, Mr. Smith?" has neither the ring of authority nor the power to amuse. What counts is the disparity between that mighty finished thing, *The Decline and Fall of the Roman Empire*, and the diminished process: children and illiterates may scribble, but not our renowned historian. He was too serious, surely; his ornamental sentences and massive buttressed paragraphs required an adept of penmanship: calligraphy, perhaps. And at the least a quill pen.

So the disjunction should amuse. It was intended to. "Still writing, Mr. Gibbon?" is a polite question merely, and would not make us laugh. As Noël Coward, with his own "talent to amuse," observed: "If you've any mind at all, Gibbon's divine *Decline and Fall* sounds pretty flimsy, no more than a whimsy. By way of contrast, on Saturday last, I went to a marvelous party. . . ."

All this by way of preface to a set of questions I think it fair to ask: Why bother with the enterprise of poetry or prose? Can writing be taught and by everyone learned? How does one place a value on such texts? Will a first-rate teacher produce a first-rate student and which are the terms of improvement—what's good, what's better, best?

Even such questions may well seem elitist, and the Duke of Gloucester has come to rule the day. For who in truth believes that language can be taught? We learned it long ago, not consciously, and by now it's closer to breathing and walking than a skill that we need to have honed. The rules that still pertain to study of a foreign language no longer apply to our own native tongue; words like "ablative" or "accusative" have been thrown out of school. Yet English is the present *lingua franca*, and very few now recognize what those words signify or how their meaning in translation has been changed. French was the language of diplomacy for centuries; not now. I don't mean by this to engage in some high-flown lament as to the lowering of standards, but only to observe that "rhetoric" is in and of itself a suspect word. Where once it meant the art of expressive speech or discourse it now seems an indulgence to avoid. Nor is a rhetorical question one that entails a reply.

In this age of electronics—with easy access to the personal computer and cell phone and home media center, television, voicemail, e-mail, and the rest—it's simple enough to get by without books. Not to mention the subsidiary skills of literacy: a knowledge of grammar and ease with articulate speech. Few adults today recite poems by heart; no one past adolescence still composes verse but those who make of it a lifelong and poorly paid vocation. Too, the art of letter writing is almost wholly defunct. The powerful have language produced for them by an oxymoronic "speechwriter"; the teleprompter is the *sine qua non* of our nightly news. Few new houses have bookshelves built in, and even the assiduous consumer will but scratch the surface of a season's available work.

Let's say—in a generous estimate—that we read a book a week and continue to do so for forty years. This would amount to 2,000 books, not a thirtieth part of the titles offered by the industry each year. Not to mention those that are reprinted and outlast a single publishing season and the shredder's blade. Or take the extreme and scholarly case; say we read five books a week for fifty years and keep them in our head and on the shelf. This would surely suggest a literate person, one of the chosen few. Yet the number's still a small one: 12,500 volumes, not the first floor of a library in any self-respecting town. And most of us don't read that much or read that long, and after twenty years or so we might as well begin again, for all we can remember of our childhood texts.

Some writers take pleasure in secondhand bookstores, those dusty upstairs rooms and barns where their predecessors molder and, perhaps, a long-sought or a half-remembered volume may be found. Some busily hunt their own work on such shelves or delight in new discovery and add to a collection. I do not. I'm haunted by the specter of these abandoned pages and those who wrote them when quick, not yet dead: a graveyard of language gone mute. It is, I think, proof negative of the folly of ambition; even Gibbon—still a household name?—is largely now remembered as the butt of another man's joke.

Nonetheless we may with justification surmise—this footnoted in *Dr. Johnson*, Volume II, by the solicitous and quasi-ubiquitous Boswell, in whose honor we here momentarily deploy an imitative Gibbonesque and *soi-disant* Johnsonian diction if not rhetoric, the *ur*-text beyond us as well as behind—that the response in due and proper course would have arrived in the affirmative, and that our author would have glanced up from his work desk, polishing his spectacles, inclining his head, smiling, weary, purse-lipped, pretending affability, secure in the foreknowledge of attainment and the satisfaction of the day's work done, and well, and perhaps already knowing that this duke so fatuously baiting him would fade into obscurity, or not so much obscurity as that particular limbo reserved for the querulous (the self-proclaimed wit and the buttonholing and lapel-pulling windy bore, the meddlesome person from Porlock), a semi-circle and half hell of indeterminate and quasi-anonymous, not to say parenthetical, identification (which Duke of Gloucester was it, after all, and old or young and in what private home and when would they discuss the scandal of the Hellfire Club?) whereas he himself, the historian *soi-même*, the great aggrieved and weary Edward Gibbon, would outlast this upright and chattering sedulous ape, survive this jape, from boot to cape caparisoned in language, lovely language, always scribble, scribble, scribble, yes indeed.

Well, that's one way to put it. Here's another. Edward Gibbon wrote a lot, and one day an acquaintance asked him why. What's the point, pal, after all? You write too much, says the Duke. Outside it's cold, it's sleeting maybe, and the poor are huddled at the coal grate by the porter's door in the alley where the night soil reeks and horse shit steams. In that corner barely visible beyond the mullioned window behold a toothless rag-wreathed creature squabbling with the dogs for scraps while in the library we light our pipes, and later on there's dancing girls, my favorite is Mimi, why bother with that quill pen, Ed, when she's so much more entertaining to tickle with this ostrich feather instead? Do pass the bottle, there's a good fellow, and sample a bit of this Stilton, I had it sent down particularly, now what were we saying? Oh yes. Let me give you a piece of advice. All work and no play keeps the devil away, and there's deviltry in Mimi and, what's the expression, you're a great one for expressions, the devil's in the details and the details are what's fun.

Some years ago I had a conversation that I carry with me, still, as a cautionary tale. I stopped a farmer—call him Everett Saunders—on his tractor in the road. The lane was dirt, little traveled, and dusty; it was July. He had been commended to me as a man who would cut wood, mow fields, do other kinds of neighborly labor for a fair price. I had more land than I could handle and was in any case incompetent at farming; I needed help. Everett recognized me also; in that village any stranger was discussed.

"You're the one they call Nick," he said, and killed the motor and lit up his pipe. Puffing, he kept silent while I blundered on about which cows I'd pasture in which field, what kind of grass I planned to plant and how much he could cut. When I said I was a college teacher and therefore—transparent excuse!—couldn't farm full time, he perked up. He had seven children; one of them was soon to enter nursing school. We had a long discussion, and he took eager part in it: the benefits of education, the value of a degree, the methodology of teaching, the particular instruction that his daughter would receive, the scholarship money available, the high cost of tuition, the risk and yield and loss. He was behind her, Everett said, behind her all the way. . . .

Emboldened by such newfound friendship, I offered a personal truth. "I'm a college teacher," I announced, "but that's not all I do. What I really love is writing. I'm a writer, I write books."

His eyes glazed. "Books," he said. He knocked his pipe bowl empty on the steering wheel. "Don't mean nothing to me." He started the tractor and left. For the five years that I worked at my three novels of the farmer's life—the Sherbrookes trilogy—I tried to remember his answer, that lack of interest and cap-tipping scorn.

Or because he is not used to playing second fiddle in any such ensemble—because *his* is the title here and *he* has commissioned the performance—Gloucester clears his throat. Loudly. To embark upon that most tedious of exercises, self-justification. Wherein he will avail himself of the very weapon of his seated adversary and also wield the pen. He will call for ink and paper and produce a monograph on ancestor worship in Mesopotamia, on weaving in the Hebrides, primogeniture in Spain. He will demonstrate once and for all that the gulf that spreads between them—the man of words and the man of action—is, to the sufficiently capacious intellect, a dimple of a ditch. He will write his own essay, compose his own speech.

It is not difficult.

It takes no time at all.

It is the sort of challenge a gentleman cannot refuse: the casual yet causal deployment of skills, the anagrammatic mustering of just the word or, as those froggies call it, *le mot juste*.

He clears his throat.

The stars, could he see them, are bright.

Matched horses stamp; breath steams.

The gutter has been sluiced.

Then, no doubt thinking better of the prospect, disheartened in advance by what he can already taste is and as the ash of half-felicitous and wholly pointless utterance, the rhetorical trope and ripe rodomontade whose tripping comeliness upon the tongue leaves triflers but the taste of tripe, that busy tinkering with language for which he does not give a tinker's damn, he lifts his white kid gloves instead from the proffered silver salver.

And shrugs himself into his greatcoat and nods at the footman, preparing to leave. For he is promised elsewhere, and time and tide won't wait. There's a matter of some urgency and—though he be too discreet to confide it—state.

Still, to have the last word is too great a temptation, and Gloucester can't resist.

Who can refuse an exit line? What actor willingly gives his back to the curtain while the curtain falls?

One final rejoinder, perhaps. One small last thing to say.

So, surrounded by his retinue and negligently, condescendingly addressing himself again to Gibbon, the Duke avers: I hunt, I ride, I court and fence and dance with more accomplishment than you. I have many achievements of which you don't dream and to which you cannot attain. When walking in the gallery or counting in the counting-house I stand or sit at ease; the highborn and the low approach and turn by turn require money, council, comfort in the battlefield or in the bed at night. To each his own, sir: you to your inkwell and I to my volume of cares. . . .

All authors have been students; many teach. We have an industry of advice on everything from investment portfolios to spiritual growth to weight loss to golf swings and how to correct what's gone wrong. Bookstores bulk large with "How to" books, and books on writing are no exception; instruction rules the day. Where there used to be just Strunk & White or Fowler's *Modern English Usage*, there are now programs to purchase, from spell-check to syntax, that guarantee improved vocabulary and increased output in thirty nanoseconds, much less thirty days.

The academy, of late, has served as patron for the writer much the way the court or wealthy individual did before. It is, I would guess—though I know of no statistical survey—the largest employer of those who make their life, if not their living, by the pen. But the poet in the Renaissance (with the exception, of course, of those gallant lords and ladies who already claimed nobility and did not sing for supper) could not imagine the practice of poetry as literally entitling; it was a business, this "singing school," and not one that granted degrees. We have moved some distance from the notion of a guild, but all those M.F.A. programs and writing festivals and writers' conferences that spring up in such profusion subscribe at least implicitly to that model of advancement: apprentice yourself to an author and earn your working papers until you too attract apprentices who come in turn to class. . . .

And though the current wave of interest in writing programs is likely to crest and diminish, the tide will rise once more. The desire of the human animal to express itself in language is inhering and enduring; from the first mark incised in stone to the contemporary microchip, we want to fashion utterance and leave it behind us for others to scan. "In the beginning was the word" may be a loose translation, but it does serve as genesis for the people of the book, and ibis-headed Thoth is god of both speech and its scribes.

The only way to learn one's art—a craftsman's paradox—is through back-breaking labor that must not seem like work. Like the dubber in a foreign-language film who most succeeds when no one knows he's around. Or like those Zen masters of the martial arts: After the body has been trained to achievement, trained so that what earlier seemed impossible is difficult, difficult habitual, and the habitual easy—at the point where everything is instinct, true mastery begins. The highest *dan* cannot be attained; the highest attainable *dan* is reached through meditation. So we have the spectacle of the ancient jiu-jitsu *sensei*, crumbled into the carapace of age, sitting on his tatami mat in the sun. And a disciple—

full of health and radiant muscularity—comes up and assumes an attack stance and says, "Master, I must kill you now," and raises the axe. But the *sensei* pulls out the rug from under his student's feet.

Therefore I urge myself to practice, trusting to the notion of perfection later on. We are all of us apprenticed to a fast-vanishing guild; the species is endangered and much mastery is specious nowadays. Hunt that old codger in the sun, I tell myself, but don't swing your axe if you find him. Look up his sleeves with reverence, and keep at a respectful distance from the mat.

Which books are *square*, when did the word come to signify *dull*, will the O.E.D. help here?

Why is the book not damned, thick and rectangular; does this suggest a conscious or unconscious inattention on the speaker's part?

Does he, I mean, not know the distinction or not bother with the difference between the rectangle and the square?

That large text and this small.

There are many more scenarios and half-fleshed possibilities; the Duke has made Mrs. Gibbon his mistress; the Duke's daughter displays a marked fondness for Gibbon but the match would be unthinkable; Gibbon has come to the Duke seeking patronage and is by this preserved response accepted or refused; the two of them were once Apostles in their shared salad days.

They have met often; they've only now been introduced; this is the start of new friendship or rupture of an old.

It would be easy enough to construct a play with these two as dramatis personae and to provide a prior or a subsequent encounter. But our patience wears thin and the rest wears away: it is only this line that remains.

For whatever the context, whatever the tone (teasing, combative, querulous?) the phrase survives. "Another damned, thick, square book!"

It's what we have that endures.

My elder brother is a doctor, and a very good one. We may have our disagreements as to politics or wine, but he is always right in matters medical and I follow his advice. Some time ago I had the habit of puns, and the more atrocious the better; no subject escaped my sonorous attention or grasping verbal reach.

An example: if the review of a novel by a *prose pro* were negative, we would have a *conte contretemps*. The contraction of "professional" to "pro" is more or less self-evident, as is the contraction of "convict" to "con." But how prosaic it would be to limit oneself to mere English, even if it be the mother tongue or bitter mother, *mère amère*; why shouldn't the contrary also prove true? To be pro or con, as in the voice-vote yea or nay, is not the same as to be a paid baseball player or a criminal who perpetrates a trick. The translation of *les cons* cannot appear in certain periodicals, but contract it to *leçons* and it seems merely instructive. English profits from the sidelong glances of such pigeon-kicking pidgin-quickening; the echoic aspect of language, its echolalic resonance, proved important to the bard of Beowulf as well as, later, John Milton and Sir Thomas Browne. It would be easy equally to play on "gibbon" as a primate's name and perhaps ancestral ape or cousin of the cadet branch, as in gorilla, orangutan, mandril, chimpanzee, a monkey who batters at Shakespeare on his battered Smith-Corona beneath the gibbous moon. . . .

Then my brother said that punning was a clinical condition, and I asked, Of what?

Of frontal lobe disorder, he said, and diseases such as tertiary syphilis—the paresis that heralds wit's end. If a patient comes into your office, he said, punning uncontrollably, you know that the patient's in trouble, and bad. I sputtered, I spluttered; he grinned. I have made few atrocious puns since.

It's fun, nevertheless, such babble; we ought to admit that. If there weren't pure pleasure in the way words edge up against each other, in the way paragraphs fit, in learning how katechresis can prove serviceable, then we'd all have to be a

higher- and bloodier-minded bunch. Because the average
wage is maybe a penny a page, or a dime each twenty hours;
the average reward is anonymity. If your name is well
enough known to be taken, then it's likely to be taken in
vain, or *misspeled*; vanity and sottishness and the deep paral-
ysis of repetition await those who truly succeed. We dream
of influence; it's effluence instead. Those who hunt success
too consciously are conscious of too little else; those to
whom it comes unbidden do its bidding soon. It's easy to
inveigh against the scribbler's rotten lot, to say we're blessed
or cursed or prophets without enough honor at home. But
there are other professions, and most professional word-
smiths could find some other job. They don't; they won't;
why not? One answer is, it's fun.

Or perhaps there's an admission here, a wry-faced yet modest avowal: the Duke doesn't care to read. He never got the
hang of it, he never acquired the taste. He has, as someone
once remarked in another context, small Latin and less
Greek. And therefore this grave history that Gibbon labored
hard to write is something of a threat to Gloucester, or at
least an implicit reproach: you understand what I fail to, sir;
what accrues to your credit lies lodged to my debt. You command language as I do the servants, you make a phrase sing
whilst I cough. A proper man—so goes the old saying—can
build a house, can plant a field and father sons and write a
book. The three first tasks present no difficulty to me, sir.
But *language*, there's the rub. . . .

From the Duke of Gloucester we may move to the Comte
de Montesquieu, whose definition of the writing life
endures: "Author: A fool who, not content with having bored
those who have lived with him, insists on tormenting the
generations to come."

In 1985 I published a book on the Beaux Arts Trio. A nonfiction study of chamber musicians, it presented a problem
of voice. I added and invented nothing but translated much.

The three artists (Isidore Cohen, violin; Bernard Green-house, cello; and Menahem Pressler, piano) were more expressive in music than in speech. Not for them the terminology of music criticism or any discussion of theory; they would demonstrate a phrase by singing or playing rather than articulating it. Greenhouse is by nature reticent and Pressler, although voluble, is not native to English. The injunction "speak in tongues" became a comic babble when I transcribed tapes. I spent a week with them at La Chaux-de-Fonds—a small town in Switzerland where they made albums for Philips Records. In conjunction with the Italian violist, Bruno Giuranna, the members of the trio recorded the two Mozart piano quartets. The engineers were Dutch, the piano tuner German. As Giuranna observed, "When musicians must discuss a piece, it's a very bad sign. You must have it in your head, of course, but play it with your heart."

Here is a verbatim rendering of discourse, from my notes and tapes. They were in rehearsal; I will not try to indicate who was speaking when.

Nun, take it from D. Wubba wubba wubba wubba. *Ich habe quasi improvisatore ici.* You follow my bowing and I follow yours. Wubba wubba. You lose the whole effect of that *piano* after playing *forte* for fourteen bars through. Last night I tried going up, today I go down—the takeover shouldn't sound as if now it's *me*—but lead up, please. I'd like a little less activity on that boobooooobooboo. Would it be too Beethoveny if you played it bumbumbum; is there a wedge on each note? No, it's the bush that burns underneath.

It's *nicht gut*. It's march music. Where do you put this accent on the phrase?

Where do you want it? On the downbeat. Then be careful of the A flat. The first five notes after the slurred note, could you start a little lighter? That sounds *vermisscht*. Did you hit the low E flat? I'm playing it; fantastic, at the end, how he takes away the chord and leaves the E flat clear for the piano. Let's try it once just as written, *nun*, from D.

Rounded off, there were fifty hours of such talk for the one completed hour of performance. The recording is, I believe, eloquent; the language clearly not. My role was to evoke the nature of the enterprise in a language faithful to the original but sufficiently distant from it to be more than mere transcription. This was a particular problem of reportage and, perhaps, extreme. But it seems to me an emblem of the novelist's ongoing task: we witness and translate.

What we choose to witness is, of course, of consequence; the sounds of a three-fingered amateur ukelele player would be less rewarding to study than those of the Beaux Arts Trio. The death of Anna Karenina has more enduring resonance than does the death of a flea. Yet Tolstoi's transcendent novel took flight from a newspaper story; James built elaborate fictions upon the chance dinner-party remark. It is seldom possible to gauge beforehand what will prove a fruitful topic or which anecdote will fire the imagination; some matters move us, some do not. The writer gleans wind-scraps; he listens whenever he can.

This is not to say the writer need do research of the spirit- or back-breaking kind. It should not be forced. Here Gibbon cannot help us much, for his entire enterprise depends upon the research done and the information accrued. Will the discerning reader note—very well, I contradict myself—that Gibbon and Gloucester now fuse at the lip? The poet and the novelist deploy a methodology separate from the historian's, and this is appropriate; we don't play tennis with a basketball or football with a bat. Nonfiction and the mass-market saga rely on data principally; fact-checking is but one component of the imagination's work. There are better roadmaps to Dublin than the novel *Ulysses*, and we would believe the snowstorm in "The Dead" if it had not snowed that day.

But if a character's a carpenter his author has to know the difference between a jig and a bandsaw; if the heroine's an

Avon lady we should know what products she sells. When we use up our store of available data—the stuff of childhood, then youth—the professional writer is left with one profession to describe. Then it grows imperative (or every book would be about its own construction) for us to practice "reach."

My argument therefore resolves into this: when the self-conscious witness casts about for subject matter, he should pay attention to the visible, audible world. Inflection is as various as fingerprints. "Another blessed thin rectangular volume!" We should train our ears and accents as do actors if we hope to play more than one part.

For finally, there are two modifiers we must finally address. Both sentences begin with an exasperated, aerated *A. Another* and *Always* bespeak true compulsion, and not so much upon the speaker's as the writer's part. What *is* it, we should ask ourselves, that keeps him keeping on? Too many trees have been leveled to furnish this ream of blank paper and realm of fool's gold; too much language has been already expended on the Roman Empire. It is enough, my *semblable*—oh, surely, much more than enough. That those who do not know their history are doomed to repeat it but compounds the problem: this repetition compulsion of sitting to the work of words day after day after day. "Another damned, thick, square book! Always scribble, scribble, scribble! Eh, Mr. Gibbon?" How is it he replies?

I write because I must.

I write for the reasons adduced here above: the fun of it, the comfort, the sense of commonality, the chance to shape what's shapeless and know what is not known.

I write because what's said is fleeting although we imagine it lasts.

And because the word "adduced" itself stands rooted in the fading past; it means "brought forward, led toward," and we will not advance as a species without the advantage of hindsight, foresight: both retrospect and prospect fused in what's composed.

For the shape of it, the sound of it though silent, the feel of the print on the page.

Out of habit too, and hard to break, the taste and smell of it, the way steam rises from my coffee cup before dawn when I wake to dream, the sixth, if only intermittently available, sense that just beyond the reach of these first five is a republic of letters where the lords of language walk.

I write because *Another* means we've been this way before.

I write in the hope that *always* means we'll go this way again.

And that you will read.